Seeking
the Wisdom
of the Heart

Seeking
the Wisdom
of the Heart

Reflections on Seven Stages
of Spiritual Development

by

Patricia Romano McGraw, Ph.D.

Bahá'í
PUBLISHING

WILMETTE, ILLINOIS

Bahá'í Publishing
415 Linden Avenue, Wilmette, Illinois 60091-2844

Copyright © 2007 by the National Spiritual Assembly
of the Bahá'ís of the United States of America
All rights reserved. Published 2007
Printed in the United States of America on acid-free paper ∞

10 09 08 07   4 3 2 1

ISBN 10: 1-931847-42-8
ISBN 13: 978-1-931847-42-1

Library of Congress Cataloging-in-Publication Data
McGraw, Patricia Romano.
    Seeking the wisdom of the heart : reflections on seven stages of
spiritual development / by Patricia Romano McGraw.
        p. cm.
    Includes bibliographical references and index.
    ISBN-13: 978-1-931847-42-1
    ISBN-10: 1-931847-42-8
    1. Self-actualization (Psychology) 2. Mental health. 3. Interper-
sonal relations. 4.
    Spiritual life. I. Title.

RA790.5.M397 2007
616.89—dc22

                                                        2006047912

To Pete,
and to our children,
and to our children's children,
and to our children's children's children

Acknowledgments

Most authors acknowledge their editors and publisher—it has become an expected formality. But my gratitude and thanks to the staff of Bahá'í Publishing goes deeper than any ritual or cliché. The first draft of this work was a failure, and I resigned from the project. The staff reacted in a way that completely shocked me. Instead of showing disappointment, they showed compassion. My heart opened and out poured this book, as much a surprise to me as to anyone.

My deepest gratitude goes to my husband Pete, who, when a one-year project turned into two, remained patient, loving, and supportive all the way.

I want to thank my friend Mike Marvin and the Bahá'í community of Olean, New York. The structure of the book, which encompasses the concepts of belief, intention, attention, and action, was first presented to their community at a public lecture. I announced to the audience my intention to write a book that included these ideas, and I promised to thank the people of Olean for inspiring me. Thanks Olean! Special thanks also go to Mike for writing the poem included in the chapter about the Valley of Wonderment.

I am indebted to two organizations that integrate scientific knowledge with spiritual principles. First, to the organization that has grown up around the movie, *What the Bleep Do We Know!?* and secondly, to the group "Mind and Life" that produces conferences and books of such exquisite scientific rigor and extraordinarily high levels of spiritual wisdom that they elevate the consciousness of the planet.

Finally, I want to thank my son Chris Romano in a special way. His insight provided the impetus for the book's beginning stages, and he was there as it drew to a close. His emotional honesty and willingness to get involved in the creative process proved to be an invaluable asset. He is not just my son; he is my friend, my advisor, and my teammate in a shared family intention to bring spiritual wisdom and light to the world.

Contents

PART ONE

Seeking the Wisdom of the Heart

Introduction

It may seem strange to you that a psychologist with twenty-four years of formal education would write a book to teach you how not to think, but I am going to do just that. As you will discover in these pages, it is possible to access a way of knowing that is smarter than "feeble reason." I have learned and continue to learn how to attune to the wisdom of my heart. In the pages that follow I will do my best to teach you to do the same by guiding you inward on a journey toward a deeper, more intimate knowledge of your own spirit, to the core of your being that is always in a state of perfect health and happiness. I will teach you how to access the wisdom of your heart, which holds within it the keys to your true happiness and fulfillment.

Most people seek happiness. And yet, for many of us, happiness is only a temporary state—fleeting, impermanent, and elusive. For some people with deep emotional scars, happiness in this lifetime may seem completely impossible. But true and lasting happiness, spiritual joy, contentment, gratitude, and love all are within you, in a potential state, at all times and under all conditions. No matter what your background or previous experiences in life may be, you can learn to access this positive state of mind. How to do it is the subject of this book.

My First Book on Trauma and Healing

I have come late in life to the task of writing books. This is my second book on emotional healing. The first book addressed emotional trauma and injury and the healing process as it unfolds in an attuned psychotherapeutic relationship. Entitled *It's Not Your Fault: How Healing Relationships Change Your Brain and Can Help You Overcome a Painful Past*, it was written after years of lecturing to many diverse audiences about emotional trauma, healing, and the brain. It explains that our brains and nervous systems grow in the context of human relationships.

It's Not Your Fault traces the development of emotional control centers within the brain and shows that the quality of the first close relationship a child has, usually with the mother, can drastically alter the future trajectory of that child's life. It explains that the most excellent type of "brain growing" relationship dynamic is a process known as "attunement" and that this process, which involves deeply focusing attention, concentrating, and getting "in sync" with another person, has a lasting positive impact throughout a person's life. Conversely, the book explains that when an attuned relationship is lacking, the emotional control centers of the brain do not grow in an ideal manner and may leave the child vulnerable to future problems with emotions and with relationships.

Attunement

"Attunement" caught on as a concept with readers who intuitively grasped its significance almost immediately. Many readers were able to quickly identify times in their lives when they felt deeply understood, supported, and cared for, and they could identify this feeling with something like the idea of another person "tuning in" to them and their inner world. They could easily recall times when attunement with a friend or a relative had allowed them to clarify a knotty problem, calm a feeling of fear or anxiety, or feel validated—in other words, to feel loved. No one has argued against the idea that receiving love from another person is good for you. And most folks have been able to identify with the concept of mutuality—the idea that when I attune to you, it is easier for you to attune to me, and when you do, not only do I benefit from the interaction, but we both receive positive benefits from this mutual interchange. These ideas make it easy to see why research in psychotherapy has for decades confirmed the notion that, regardless of the school or method of psychotherapy employed, the strength of the therapeutic relationship often has the biggest positive impact on the outcome of the therapy.

The premise of *It's Not Your Fault* is that the processes of attunement that foster brain development occur unconsciously and very early in the developmental process. Despite their "unseen" nature, these positive relationship dynamics leave a lasting mark. And conversely, "unseen" childhood traumas such as abandonment and neglect have an equally indelible negative impact. Physical, emotional, and sexual abuse similarly leave their neurobiological imprint. In *It's Not Your Fault* a woman named Kim describes aspects of her own childhood traumas and then discusses her healing journey, which occurred over many years in an attuned psychotherapeutic relationship with me. As Kim describes her life experiences, I attempt to link those experiences to some of the unconscious brain dynamics that appear to be occurring as she heals.

It's Not Your Fault was an attempt to simplify and make accessible to the general reader some of neurobiologist Alan Schore's work. His classic text titled *Affect Regulation and the Origin of the Self* (1994) is a masterpiece of intellectual prowess showing that relationships are not just nice "add-ons" to biological growth and development. They are absolutely central to emotional health and well-being from the first moments of life all the way through the life span. In fact, one woman who read *It's Not Your Fault* commented that reading it helped her to become more assertive in her relationships. She said, "It's a lot easier to tell my boss to quit yelling at me all the time when I know he's not just making me uncomfortable, he's hurting my brain!"

Of course, this kind of brain talk can go too far, and the notion that we can separate what is "physical" from what is "mental" or "emotional" is fast becoming passé even in many scientific circles. As my discussion will explain, I now understand myself to be "mindbodyspirit" all in one, and in this equation spirit is both the ground of my being and the goal of my being. Emotional life is closely linked with seemingly "spiritual" concepts like love, virtue, and awareness of our inner being. Physical health is closely associated with emotional health. Recent research on stress reduction and the positive impact of complimentary and alternative medicine approaches to healing the body clearly demonstrates that mind, body, and spirit cannot truly be thought of as separate spheres.

It's Not Your Fault has been very well received. I continue to lecture about its subject matter to audiences around the country. I find that all demographic groups—from white college students in the most prestigious colleges to Native Americans on reservations, from managers of multimillion-dollar corporations to the poorest of the poor in mental health treatment, the young, the old, and everyone in between—all seem to identify with the concept that being deeply understood is a powerful positive force. And unfortunately it seems that very few of us have consistent access to someone who deeply understands us. On top of that, we all seem to have suffered some form of traumatic emotional injury, or at least we all seem to know someone else close to us who has. My experience in traveling and talking with folks in many parts of the United States over the past three years tells me that we are all on a healing journey of one form or another.

In *Seeking the Wisdom of the Heart,* I write about the fact that the healing journey does not end. Our life on earth is really a continuous process of finding our way home to our spiritual core, where true happiness awaits us. Readers of my previous book will find that some of the themes that began in *It's Not Your Fault* are taken to a deeper level.

What Sustains Me?

Certainly, the science I discussed in *It's Not Your Fault* and the key element of attunement played an important role in the process of Kim's moving from a position of feeling worthless and actively suicidal to her current status as a successful, energetic mother and professional. Still, as the later chapters of *It's Not Your Fault* alluded, there has to be more to the story.

Kim was not always easy to work with. Often, I was attuning to her and she was unable to reciprocate. Sometimes she acted out her emotional scars by doing self-destructive things, by being negative and threatening to give up, or by being angry and full of rage. At these times and other times, too, she would ask, "Why do you put up with me? Aren't you tired of me yet?" "When are you going to see that I am not worth the effort?" Over and over again she would ask, "Why do you do this? Why do you do this work?"

I would answer, "Because I *choose* to."

"And why do you choose to?" she would ask.

"Because I believe that is my purpose in life, to choose to act to help others when I can. Besides, it isn't difficult, because I perceive you to be a wonderful woman. I can see within you all sorts of untapped potential that is just waiting to bloom. That is what I see when I look at you, that is what I pay *attention* to."

As I have lectured about *It's Not Your Fault,* this question has come up again and again about me and about my own beliefs and my choice to try to help someone who was suffering from so many problems. Why did I do it? The questions reflect curiosity about the other person in this two-person relationship dynamic I experienced with Kim. She was healing, and her interior life was changing. That much was clear. But if I was selling the idea that relationships are key, what about me? What was going on inside of myself that sustained me when Kim was difficult? As I mulled over these issues, I realized a bigger issue underlies these questions, an issue perhaps we all share. How can one love when the loving is difficult? What is the source of this energy that one gives out to others?

Personal Responsibility

The second question that came up again and again concerned the issue of personal responsibility. If it's not your fault that you were mistreated as a child, is it also not your fault if you mistreat your own children? If it's not your fault that you suffered mental injuries as a soldier in wartime battle that left you with a reservoir of anger and hatred, is it also not your responsibility if you come home and beat your wife and your children to vent this anger? If it's not your fault that you were sexually abused as a child, is it not your responsibility if you abuse other children while you are still a child or when you become an adult? In other words, given our life experiences, where does our personal responsibility for our own life begin and end? Shouldn't people be held responsible for the consequences of their actions? Don't people have free will? Can't they get over the past and choose to live in ways that are not bound to their past?

Of course they can, and the purpose of this book is to explore how. These ideas are, for me, the inevitable ethical downbeat to the upbeat of my first book. Your life experiences do influence you in ways that are not your fault and are not under your control. These experiences leave their imprint. But dealing with these issues and growing spiritually, regardless of your life circumstances, are your responsibility.

Healing When There Is No One To Help You

A number of important issues have emerged from the ideas in *It's Not Your Fault*. First there is the issue of inner life itself—in this case, my own inner life and the role it played and continues to play in my relationships. And then there is also the issue of personal responsibility. How exactly do you take responsibility for dealing with inner scars, or trigger spots, that throw you into negative emotional states? And third, there is the idea of having someone to help you heal. What if you decide to take responsibility for your inner healing and no one is around to help you? What about healing that does not necessarily include a close relationship with another living person? Is it possible to attune to the healing energy in the universe directly? Does one have to have a human "conduit" for others to receive this energy?

At one of my bookstore presentations, a woman raised her hand and said in a thick New York accent touched with no small measure of sarcasm, "Look, Doc, I read the book. What you said about being in this wonderful state of healing attunement with your patient for years and years is all well and good, but I don't have all those years *left* in my life, and I don't have *you*. So now what do I do?"

Lots of other folks talked about the difficulty of finding someone to connect with them on their healing journey. Attunement as a concept is fine, but it is a duet. What is the answer when there is no one to do the duet with you and no one in your life can love and understand you? Where can you go to find direction? Is it possible to heal without anyone to help guide and direct you?

Over the last three years I have been reading and researching and attending conferences with these three questions in mind: First, the issue of inner life and the role it plays in happiness and well-being, including the ability to love others; second, the issue of personal responsibility for one's inner life, regardless of life's outward circumstances; and third, the issue of attunement to the healing spiritual energies of the universe and the availability of this energy to be accessed directly without another person being present.

The Search for Answers

To prepare to write this book, I made an outline and then spent over a year reading more than one hundred books on all sorts of different aspects and approaches to spirituality, from Buddhism and mindfulness to biophysical approaches that focus on the heart. I read "new age" literature, ancient texts, and various scriptures, and I listened to Native American stories. I searched far and wide. All of the references listed at the end of this volume were part of my search. I found many ideas very illuminating, and I met many people on the road who shared their thoughts and ideas with me. Then I sat down and wrote. First I used the original outline, then, abandoning it completely, I kept writing and rewriting, changing the title, changing the focus. Finally it was time to send something to the publisher. I pressed the "send" button of my e-mail system and waited for the response. Eventually a response came. Basically, the editors responded, as kindly as they could, with comments that added up to "yuck." The manuscript was an incoherent jumble—confused, disjointed, and out of sync. One of the comments from the editors was "I don't know what this book is about."

I Quit

So, logically, I quit. I abandoned the project and felt quite embarrassed and upset that I had failed so miserably when I had tried so hard. After I quit, I had the urge to write in my journal and try to "download" some of the insights and wisdom I had gained so that I could go on to other projects. I would write, if not for others, to satisfy myself and record something of what I had learned from my experience.

One of the texts I discovered during my wide search was the Seven Valleys, a Bahá'í treatise on spiritual growth that had been sitting on my bookshelf for years, unopened. I became fascinated with it, as my journal entries reflect. I noticed that so much of what I had learned from my reading seemed to be very closely associated with the ideas expressed in the Seven Valleys. I realized that just one or two phrases from Bahá'u'lláh in that small book seemed to capture an idea that secular authors took hundreds of pages to cover.

Beginning a Spiritual Journal of My Heart

Just for the sake of my own spiritual journey and to clear my head after the upsetting experience of my failed book project, I began writing with a fountain pen in a bound journal. I took my time. I began to reflect on just tiny sentences or small passages within the Seven Valleys, and I began to write down these reflections, organizing them within the general framework of moving from one valley of spiritual development to the next. Lo and behold, the book I had been trying to write with my "head" began to emerge, as if on its own, from my "heart." I dared not speak of what was happening while it was happening. I was having too much fun doing this journaling and finding it to be "too easy" to consider that I might be writing a book (a process that had previously been a kind of mental agony for me). Now, when I look back on my earlier attempts, I find plenty to chuckle about. The Seven Valleys is always urging us to abandon what it calls our "feeble reason" and rely on the inspiration of the spirit, an idea I obviously find hard to take in.[1]

Creating My Own Reality?

The working title of the first version of this book—which, in retrospect, was clearly a "feeble reason" attempt—was "Creating Your Own Reality" because I felt that the thoughts I had to share would begin to shed light on how our inner beliefs, choices, perceptions, and actions create our experience of reality. But then I began to reflect on how these words could be used against me in my work.

I practice forensic psychology, meaning that I testify in court cases involving the law and mental health issues. For instance, I might evaluate someone for competency to stand trial or for criminal responsibility. Sometimes I evaluate those who have committed crimes to determine whether or not mental illness affected their judgment at the time of the crime, and so on. I began to imagine a court scene in some future case when the opposing attorney might hold up both of the books I had written: *It's Not Your Fault* and *Creating Your Own Reality*. I could see the attorney in my mind's eye, looking at me with sarcasm saying, "Ah, I see, doctor, that not only do you not think people are responsible for their actions—as we see in your *first* book—but you also believe that we are all insane and that you are a proponent of this insanity as you have described in your *second* book!"

Obviously, I don't think we all create our own reality in the sense of concrete objective things. I believe in the "reality" of tables and chairs and stones and trees. And of course there is a social reality, too, and a cultural reality, and all sorts of agreed upon notions of what is a rational perception in the sense that a court of law would allow. And of course I don't think everyone is insane in the way I define it in my work and in relation to the law. Rather, the reality to which I refer should perhaps be termed your inner experience, or your interpretation of what happens to you. It is your personal "slant" on everyday life. One of my goals is to help you question your beliefs and perceptions. Your own particular "slant" may be just that—a "slant"—just one choice among many choices that are available to you at all times. I have come to understand that as my own spiritual development unfolds, my perceptions change, my reactions change, and my reality, in fact, changes.

As you will see, regardless of how any of us appears to the world, and regardless of outward circumstances, our inner world—the life of our spirit—can and does exert a determining influence on our inner experience of happiness, contentment, and fulfillment. In other words, at the higher levels of spiritual development, you can experience the deepest happiness regardless of your outward circumstances. Another one of the working titles for the book I wrote and then abandoned was "Living from the Inside Out."

Living from the Inside Out

When I speak to audiences about the ability of the inward to trump outward circumstances, I am fond of citing 'Abdu'l-Bahá's description of his time in prison. 'Abdu'l-Bahá (1844–1921) is the son of Bahá'u'lláh (1817–92), the prophet and founder of the Bahá'í Faith. The Bahá'í Faith began in Persia (present-day Iran) about 150 years ago. Bahá'u'lláh, the son of a wealthy aristocratic family, was destined for a life of comfort and respect among the Muslim leaders of his country. However, when he declared his mission as the next voice of God upon earth, he was banished from his homeland and spent the majority of the rest of his life in prison. His son 'Abdu'l-Bahá was only a small boy when all of this began. As a result, he knew no other life but that of imprisonment, torture, derision, physical deprivation, and all the earthly agonies that you can imagine would accompany prison life 150 years ago. And yet this is what 'Abdu'l-Bahá said about his time in prison:

> *I myself was in prison forty years—one year alone would have been impossible to bear—nobody survived that imprisonment more than a year! But, thank God, during all those forty years I was supremely happy! Every day, on waking, it was like hearing good tidings, and every night infinite joy was mine. Spirituality was my comfort, and turning to God was my greatest joy.*[2]

So I always ask audiences, what would I think if I were to be asked to do a forensic psychological evaluation of 'Abdu'l-Bahá while he was in prison? Would I conclude that he must be "crazy" to feel "supremely happy" in such miserable circumstances? Would I conclude that his assertions that he "conversed with God" were psychotic? Would I suggest that he needed psychotherapy or medication so that he could reenter "reality"?

Clearly, we are beings of both a spiritual and material nature. However, in the American culture in which I live today, I often find it hard to keep my spiritual focus. I find so much to distract me, so many ways to put my material existence ahead of my spiritual life.

If you finish this book, you will know more than you ever wanted to know about what goes on inside my head as my feeble reason struggles to stay in control of the spiritual wisdom of my heart. Sometimes, the whole struggle seems so ridiculous it is humorous. At least it seems that way to me. I don't mind a good laugh at myself. It seems pretty ridiculous when my head tries to solve problems while my heart quietly waits for the noise inside to settle. Then the heart quietly speaks—simply, honestly, directly.

Calm Down

I often tell a story about this difficulty of turning inward. The story, like all the stories I share in this book, is true. It happened to me just this way.

About ten years ago I went through a very emotionally difficult time. The stress wore on and on, and after a time, many months had gone by and I hadn't even been able to pray. Throughout my life, since I was very young, I have always relied on prayer, so the situation became agonizing for me. I resolved to take whatever measures were needed to fix it. I thought, "Where can I go to pray? Where is the place on earth (well, in the United States, because this was a budget-minded spiritual quest) that is closest to God? I remembered Glacier National Park in Wyoming. It was winter, and sure enough, I found that a ski club in my area was planning to go there. "Aha!" I said. "I'll go there. That will do it. I always feel close to God on top of the mountains in the snow." Besides, I knew Glacier National Park to be a place of immense beauty. "You've got to feel close to God there," I reasoned.

So I packed my skis, plunked down a fair chunk of change to pay for the trip, and set off with a group of complete strangers to find God. I began to get a little worried when I kept overhearing the phrase "extreme skiing" and noticed most of my fellow skiers carried walkie-talkies in case they became lost in the wilderness or got buried under an avalanche. "Oh, great," I thought. "I am already lost and buried, and I haven't even seen the snow yet!"

Well, finally after quite a number of adventures that had nothing to do with my spiritual quest, I found myself on top of a gorgeous mountain, all alone in the deep, powdery snow. I plopped myself down, looked up to the heavens, and said, "Well, now what?"

And, indeed I heard the voice I took to be that of my Creator speaking loudly and clearly. It spoke but two words, and the message was unmistakable: "CALM DOWN."

"What?" I screamed out loud.

"Calm down."

"That's IT? Just 'CALM DOWN'?" I asked.

And then, again, and louder this time, "Calm down!"

"Humph," I said. "Well, I never! I spend all this money and come all this way, and all I hear is 'calm down.'"

And then, in case I missed the message, I heard it a third time: "CALM DOWN!" This time loud, authoritative, maybe even annoyed.

I took it to mean that I was to calm down that inner chatter. Well, as the saying goes, the rest is history. Whatever "calm down" meant, it was the start of a new phase in my spiritual journey. Learning what it means to "calm down" and how to apply this understanding in my daily life became an ongoing effort, and I am still trying to calm down. In the pages that follow, I am afraid you will encounter plenty of my silly inner chatter blathering away over the quiet inner voice of my spirit, still trying to get through.

What you will find in these pages reflects the state, such as it is, of my own spiritual journey. Don't worry; nothing in here will intimidate you. I will be at all times focusing and reflecting on quotations taken directly from the Seven Valleys. The entire text of the Seven Valleys is included in the appendix. I encourage you to read it in its entirety at your leisure. This is a Bahá'í sacred text. Bahá'u'lláh promises that within each word of his inspired writings one can find an ocean of meaning. Therefore, please be very clear that my writing represents only my reflections on Bahá'u'lláh's words and on my own life and in no way whatsoever represents any kind of authoritative statement of the Bahá'í position on these ideas.

This book shares passages from my personal journal and my reflections on what I am learning about my spiritual journey and nothing more. Still, I am hoping you may find within my struggles to progress spiritually something of your own struggle. Maybe you will identify with my difficulty in simply focusing my attention inward. Maybe you, like me, find life so busy and out of balance that days can go by without a pause even to reflect for a second. Perhaps, like me, you can remember a time when you had a moment of inward awareness that seared like a laser light into your heart and soul, where that awareness remains as a spiritual guidepost, beckoning you back to that moment of clarity and happiness.

The Fountain of Youth

I have often talked with my husband about this idea of the spiritual journey. One morning he startled me by suddenly exclaiming, "Why, that is the fountain of youth!" (No, it wasn't the same as the "calm down" voice, but it was close.) You will notice as my musings continue that my husband is generally more spiritually perceptive than I am. I have learned to resist the urge to just dismiss his ideas offhand. He so often makes sense just when I think he is totally out of his mind! Nevertheless, it is always a struggle for those of more lowly spiritual ascent (like me) to cope with the insightful (like him). On the morning that he mentioned the fountain of youth, I looked at him with knitted eyebrows and that "what are you talking about?" face while I attempted with my voice to sound fascinated.

He continued, "When you find your spiritual journey, you have found the fountain of youth, because if you continue the journey, you never grow old. You just get deeper and deeper into this place of spiritual joy, and you seem to get younger and more lively and glowing as the years go by. That is what the fountain of youth is—to be filled with life. The spiritual journey that begins here will even go on into the next life. The journey begins here, but it never ends. That is the true fountain of youth!"

"Oh," I said, humbled. If only my husband were inclined to type, I thought, I could have just passed this whole writing project on to him. But, no, there is a reason, I am sure, that I was struggling to write this second book. This work is part of my own spiritual journey.

Disclaimers

Language fails in the face of the ineffable. The adherents of the religions with which I am familiar have not developed a common vocabulary and tend to vie with one another for superiority or exclusive knowledge of the spirit. For me, facing this task of trying to write a book about spiritual matters that is nondenominational is a difficult thing. I will be using language that I am familiar with. Please note that the general concepts apply to all religions and spiritual pathways.

Truth is truth, no matter where you find it. I will use the word "God." In this culture—meaning the United States today—this word is the most common usage for a variety of names for the Creator. The Great Spirit, Alláh, Jehovah, Yahweh, and other names refer to the idea of a spiritual energy that is positive, loving, and the sum of all there is.

The Bahá'í Faith, to which I belong, adheres to principles I embrace with all my heart and soul. It promotes the concept that all religions are one. All the world's peoples are one. Bahá'u'lláh wrote, "The earth is but one country, and mankind its citizens."[3] Please do not confuse my reliance on the Bahá'í scriptures with any claim to exclusivity, superiority, or conflict with other spiritual pathways. Unity is the goal. Peace to all is the aim. According to the Bahá'í teachings, if I were to create any conflict or dissension with others based on my religious beliefs, it would be better if I were to have no beliefs at all, no religion at all.

Spiritual practice is a healing medicine for all of humanity's ills. I hope that you will honor my intention and not use any of these imperfect thoughts and reflections of mine to contribute in any way at all to negativity on the planet. Goodness knows, we have plenty of that already. If these thoughts and reflections do not help to soothe, comfort, enlighten, or guide, please toss this book away, but I urge you to continue to turn inward to the wisdom of your own heart and spirit. This is where true knowledge and love abide.

I believe that the sacred scriptures of all the religions of the world are endowed with spiritual inspiration. But while all spiritual pathways are essentially and ultimately one, I cannot possibly speak of all of them at once in a book of this kind. As I have been saying for years to my clients, I believe that what is most deeply personal is most universal. The more deeply we humans go into the depths of our own hearts, the closer we come to that vein of life and truth that unites us all. To be honest with yourself and others touches hearts. In fact, I believe it is the only way to touch hearts.

Outline of the Chapters

I begin the first chapter by discussing the concept of states of consciousness and by showing that belief, intention, attention, and action play pivotal roles in moving you from lower states of consciousness to higher states that are associated with spiritual enlightenment, lasting happiness, health, and service to humanity. Consciousness itself is difficult to define, so I will rely on examples and personal stories to make my points. As for the idea of moving to lower states of consciousness from higher ones—well, that, unfortunately, happens all too easily and without any effort. As soon as my effort to progress spiritually lags or my attention wanders, my consciousness will fall like a rock to the baser material levels.

In Part 2, my own inner journey begins. I invite you to join me. I will be using the Seven Valleys, a mystic text on spiritual development, as a guide and a focus for my meditations. I will continue through each of the Seven Valleys, and within each stage I will include four subsections: (1) Some of the original text written by Bahá'u'lláh about the spiritual experiences in that valley, and then (2) my journal entries in response to it. Each subsection will also include (3) questions to ponder regarding the issues raised in the journal. Sometimes meditation exercises or other activities are included. Before I move out of a valley and on to the next one, I will include (4) a summation and evaluation of the main points I have learned from studying that valley and by focusing on the issues of belief, intention, attention, and action. I will try to bring myself to account, assessing what I have learned and what I need to work on in order to progress.

You may notice that as I progress through the valleys, the chapters become shorter and less elaborate. This is because the later valleys deal with the highest levels of development, and my own spiritual limitations prevent me from saying more. In the conclusion, I will return to the three questions I have posed that have arisen from *It's Not Your Fault.* I will do my best to reflect on what this journey has meant for me and how it has changed my life.

These pages trace a process of my own personal transformation. My intention is to show you a process. The content is much less important, I think, than the process. I am hoping that by being honest with you about my own inner life, I may be able to help you find the courage and the interest to face and examine your own inner life. I am trying to share with you the idea that anyone and everyone can do this. It is not a process that is only for sages or monks or philosophers or intellectuals. I believe spiritual development is a process that is fundamental to everyone's life. My goal is to make this process clearer and more accessible. I am hoping that as you see me encounter obstacles to inner awareness you will identify with these obstacles in some way and will be encouraged to press forward.

You will see that at first, as I begin to turn my attention to my own inner life, I am terrible at it! I can't sit still, I can't concentrate. I become fascinated with even the most mundane things (such as vacuuming, even though I hate to vacuum). Then you will see me make some small progress. You will see the progress reverse itself, then jump forward, then back again. Moment to moment we humans have the capacity to make choices, to turn our attention this way or that, and from the progression of these moment by moment choices, life unfolds.

You will see that as I turn my attention to my own heart, I gain a clearer understanding of how my beliefs, attention, intention, and actions are flowing from my inner reality. You will see me in the process of change, as I become more acutely aware of how my perception is influenced by my own emotional states, my personal scars, my expectations of others, and many other things that are part of my own inner life. You will see how I sometimes "project" this inner "stuff" onto others, and you will see how my lack of inner awareness and failure to face my own truths can cause conflict with other people—even people I love.

I come to this task with a fair amount of—well—chagrin, I guess. I have no real desire to make my inner thoughts so public. But after my long struggle to find a way to share the process of "inner-to-outer" reality, I could not find another way to capture the process. The process is key. It is not which passages of scripture I am reading or what I am saying to myself about these passages that really holds promise for you as you read. It is what will go on inside *you* that counts. I trust and believe that you have the same capacity I have, the capacity to know yourself intimately. I trust and believe that this awareness of yourself can grow with practice and the determination to focus your time and energy in this endeavor. I know from my own experience that if you take the time and make the effort, you will be greatly rewarded.

So this book is meant to create for you a different type of experience than you have reading most books. I do not intend for you to just sit and read right through it. I am hoping that you will relate to the book in a way that will cause you to ask yourself questions: What do I hold most dear in my heart? How is this intention affecting my life every day? Where is my attention focused at this very moment? How is this focus affecting my life? What happens to my outer life when I take more responsibility for my inner life? Do I even know about my inner life at all? For some folks, their inner experience is a kind of "black box." They focus their attention on incessant activity and busyness and never even take the first glance "inside." I have had folks tell me, "I don't want to go there."

I am inviting you to go there. I am going there too. I am sharing my experiences in the hope that you will follow the pattern and begin or intensify your own inward spiritual journey. The quest is to seek the wisdom of your own heart. An absolute, unguarded, and unvarnished search for truth will be the beacon that will guide us. The promise is that within my heart and yours, true and lasting happiness await. Hidden potential lies, waiting to be discovered. This is the journey that doesn't end. As Bahá'u'lláh says, "The Word of God is the king of words and its pervasive influence is incalculable. . . . The Word is the master key for the whole world, inasmuch as through its potency the doors of the hearts of men, which in reality are the doors of heaven, are unlocked."[4]

Belief, Intention, Attention, and Action

Thou hast asked Me concerning the nature of the soul. Know, verily, that the soul is a sign of God, a heavenly gem whose reality the most learned of men hath failed to grasp, and whose mystery no mind, however acute, can ever hope to unravel. It is the first among all created things to declare the excellence of its Creator, the first to recognize His glory, to cleave to His truth, and to bow down in adoration before Him. If it be faithful to God, it will reflect His light, and will, eventually, return unto Him. If it fail, however, in its allegiance to its Creator, it will become a victim to self and passion, and will, in the end, sink in their depths.

—BAHÁ'U'LLÁH, *GLEANINGS*

Belief in the Dual Nature of Man

I must begin my discussion of spiritual development with the question of what it is and why it is necessary. The quotation above from Bahá'u'lláh describes my understanding of the relationship of my soul to this physical life and tells me that my true nature is good. I have a soul that has the potential to reflect the light of God Himself. However, the quotation also says that I have choices. I can be faithful to God or not. To be faithful in this sense requires, first of all, that I believe there is a God and that I believe I have a soul that is based on His qualities. So belief is the foundation. I also have to make a choice, create my own intention, to be faithful to God and to follow the promptings of my soul that lead me toward greater and greater spiritual knowledge and understanding— or not.

Human beings, I believe, are really spiritual beings who have become "associated with" a material body. The soul is not *in* the body per se, nor is it outside the body, nor does it hover somewhere between heaven and earth. Rather, spirit is the goal of our being, and it is the ground of our being. Spirit in theological terms is both "transcendent" and "immanent." Spirit pervades all creation, and in fact nothing that has existence is devoid of spirit. It is so hard to describe these things in words.

I will let someone much more spiritually advanced than I am tell you about the relationship of the soul to the body in his own words. 'Abdu'l-Bahá—the son of Bahá'u'lláh, the prophet and founder of the Bahá'í Faith—is considered by Bahá'ís to be the perfect exemplar for living a spiritual life. When asked, "What is the wisdom of the spirit's appearing in the body?" he shared the following:

> *The wisdom of the appearance of the spirit in the body is this: the human spirit is a Divine Trust, and it must traverse all conditions, for its passage and movement through the conditions of*

existence will be the means of its acquiring perfections. So when a man travels and passes through different regions and numerous countries with system and method, it is certainly a means of his acquiring perfection, for he will see places, scenes and countries, from which he will discover the conditions and states of other nations. He will thus become acquainted with the geography of countries and their wonders and arts; he will familiarize himself with the habits, customs and usages of peoples; he will see the civilization and progress of the epoch; he will become aware of the policy of governments and the power and capacity of each country. It is the same when the human spirit passes through the conditions of existence: it will become the possessor of each degree and station. Even in the condition of the body it will surely acquire perfections.[1]

'Abdu'l-Bahá refers to passing "through" existence and says that within existence there are different "degrees" and "stations." He says that the soul becomes the "possessor" of each degree and station as it passes through the various stages. Another way of describing these stations and degrees is to call them different levels of consciousness.

The quotation above explains that the soul itself is educated here in this physical world. 'Abdu'l-Bahá says it "acquires perfections," and as it does so, it advances and "traverses all conditions." As you learn and acquire spiritual knowledge, you move "up" and are constantly growing, developing, and moving closer and closer to God. This process begins here on earth. Our physical development reflects this process. We are born infants, unable to do anything for ourselves. We are entirely dependent on our parents for survival. As we grow and develop, we acquire knowledge and we advance mentally, socially, and spiritually too.

Intention and Choice

'Abdu'l-Bahá says that there is a dynamic relationship between God and humankind that works as follows. When a person chooses to do so, he or she can align with God and shine the light of God into the world. Then this light will not only transform the one who is doing the shining, it will begin to transform the world too. It will illumine it, enlighten it, and "attract like a magnet" good things to its light. If you are giving the light out into the world, the light comes pouring back at you, further enlightening you, allowing you to shine more brightly, then pouring back on you even more strongly, and making you even brighter, and so on, and so on.

Many world religions call the highest levels of consciousness "enlightenment." The most enlightened beings on planet Earth have been the Prophets of God—among them Buddha, Krishna, Zoroaster, Abraham, Moses, Christ, Muḥammad—and from the Bahá'í Faith, the Báb* and Bahá'u'lláh. These beings are perfect mirrors of the Spirit of

---

* The Báb, meaning literally *The Gate*, was the title assumed by Siyyid 'Alí-Muḥammad (20 October 1819–9 July 1850) after declaring His mission in S̲h̲íráz in 1844. The Báb's station is twofold: He is a Manifestation of God and the founder of the Bábí Faith, and He is the herald of Bahá'u'lláh.

God, which is why Bahá'ís refer to them as "Manifestations of God." They manifest, or possess, all the attributes and qualities of God and yet appear in human form.

None of us mere mortals can ever achieve the level of pure spiritual enlightenment that the Manifestations of God achieve because they have two basic natures, one Divine and one human. We mortals have only a human nature that includes the possibility of becoming "divine" in the small "d" sense. 'Abdu'l-Bahá says humans who choose not to develop their divine trust can become "inferior to the inhabitants of the lower animal kingdom."[2] So the element of choice is key. We must believe that our true nature is that of a spiritual being having a material existence, and then we must choose to try to learn and advance our level of consciousness. That is what spiritual development is all about.

But why bother with spiritual development? This is a logical question. What is the payoff? Well, you will have to try it yourself to truly understand. You see, as you progress within your spiritual development process, your perceptions about yourself and others will shift. You will experience this shift yourself. I can't really talk "about" it—it is something you have to experience. That is why I decided to use my own journal as a vehicle and to invite you to try to experience the transformative effects of spiritual practice yourself. Trying to explain it is like trying to explain the taste of ice cream or like trying to taste it by looking at a picture. Talking *about* something is not the same as actually *experiencing* something. Consciousness is an experience.

You are already familiar with the experience of different states of consciousness. You enter different states of consciousness each day when you awaken, go to sleep, become alert, feel drowsy, and so forth. When you shift from one state of consciousness to another, your perceptions change, your experience changes, you might say that your reality changes. Consider the following quotation from Bahá'u'lláh:

As to thy question concerning the worlds of God. Know thou of a truth that the worlds of God are countless in their number, and infinite in their range. None can reckon or comprehend them except God, the All-Knowing, the All-Wise. Consider thy state when asleep. Verily, I say, this phenomenon is the most mysterious of the signs of God amongst men, were they to ponder it in their hearts. Behold how the thing which thou hast seen in thy dream is, after a considerable lapse of time, fully realized. Had the world in which thou didst find thyself in thy dream been identical with the world in which thou livest, it would have been necessary for the event occurring in that dream to have transpired in this world at the very moment of its occurrence. Were it so, you yourself would have borne witness unto it. This being not the case, however, it must necessarily follow that the world in which thou livest is different and apart from that which thou hast experienced in thy dream. This latter world hath neither beginning nor end. It would be true if thou wert to contend that this same world is, as decreed by the All-Glorious and Almighty God, within thy proper self and is wrapped up within thee. It would equally be true to maintain that thy spirit, hav-

ing transcended the limitations of sleep and having stripped it-self of all earthly attachment, hath, by the act of God, been made to traverse a realm which lieth hidden in the innermost reality of this world. Verily I say, the creation of God embraceth worlds besides this world, and creatures apart from these crea-tures. In each of these worlds He hath ordained things which none can search except Himself, the All-Searching, the All-Wise. Do thou meditate on that which We have revealed unto thee, that thou mayest discover the purpose of God, thy Lord, and the Lord of all worlds. In these words the mysteries of Divine Wis-dom have been treasured.[3]

Attention

The passage above explains that many realities are open to us, but accessing them requires effort. We are told to meditate and to try to discover the "mysteries" that are hid-den within the words. It is interesting to think about the fact that the quote says the hidden mysteries are not far off in some other land or some other place. They are not "out there." They are within all of us. We just need to pay atten-tion to them and discover them. How to do that is closely tied not only to our own beliefs and our choice to do so, but also to our ability to pay attention.

To begin to discover the "clues" to the mystery of the realities that are wrapped up and hidden within us, it will be useful to think deeply about attention and its role in creating the stories of our lives that we take to be reality. Let's take a look at a hypothetical example and see how attention works.

The Flashlight of Attention

Let's imagine that my business partner, Dave, and I are walking together to a strange part of town. It is late at night and pitch black outside. We are going to inspect a building to see if we want to buy it and set up an office together there. We have been told the building is old but in "good shape," and we have been told that we can have it at a good price that includes all the furnishings left inside.

Dave and I imagine being in this office together for many years, so we both want to be careful to make a good decision. We are surprised by the low price, which seems almost too good to be true, so we don't want to wait until morning to take a look at it. We agree to meet at the building and to have coffee after our inspection to make a decision about whether to purchase it.

We arrive at the dark building together with our flashlights. The only things we can see on this dark, moonless night are those things that are illumined by our flashlights. Dave and I greet each other, and we agree that I will take the first look while he waits outside for safety's sake. I take the key, open the door to the old building, and from the doorway I shine my flashlight ahead of my footsteps. Dave is waiting behind me and can't see a thing.

As I shine my light on the floor, I see an old plank floor that is full of dust. A mouse scampers past my beam of light. Along the floorboards I see peeling paint. I see the legs of old, dusty pieces of furniture, and I smell something strange, something I don't recognize as a familiar smell. I put the smell together in my mind with the dirt, the peeling paint, and the mouse, and I deduce that the smell must be coming from mold. I conclude that this is a dirty, filthy, disease-ridden place that I would never in a million years want to rent for an office. I back out quickly, having made up my mind, and I allow Dave to enter with his flashlight.

While Dave inspects the premises, I am aware that I have paid attention to what I have seen, and based on my beliefs about these perceptions, I have formed an opinion, and based on that opinion I have made a decision. If you were to ask me at that moment whether or not my opinion is correct, factual, and based on objective evidence, I would say "certainly it is." I believe I have *proof* that this is a terrible place.

When Dave walks into the building he shines his flashlight toward the ceiling. He does not shine it on the floor. He sees a large, antique crystal chandelier, obviously very ornate and expensive. He shines his light around the edges of the ceiling and sees fancy molding from the turn of the century. It needs paint, but it is exquisite. He drops his light a bit further and sees an old grand piano sitting in the corner of the room. (Its legs are the dusty legs I had seen.) It is a Steinway— a musical treasure! The piano alone, regardless of the age, is worth the price of the building. Dave notices that someone has been taking care of it. It has a faint glow and he smells wood polish.

Dave steps away from the doorway and says, "Wow, no question here about what the decision is." I quickly answer, "Yup, it's obvious to me too." And we go to the coffee shop for our discussion.

We have just experienced two different realities. We have come to two completely different assessments of the situation. The only thing that differed was our attention to the details of the present moment and the "story" that we created in our minds based on those details. I saw dirt and peeling paint and created a future story of misery and disease. Dave saw antique treasures and created a story of material prosperity, excitement, happiness, and joy—music even. Which of us is "right"? Which of us is "wrong"? Is there a right and a wrong?

Living on Two Different Planets

Imagine in your mind for a moment the kind of discussion that Dave and I might have back at the restaurant where we decided to have coffee. Ask yourself, have you ever had a discussion with someone in which you felt as if you and the other person were from different planets? Have you ever wondered how in the world people can be so stupid or why in the world some people seem to lack common sense?

Back at the coffee shop, Dave says, "Well, clearly we need to grab this thing before someone else sees what is available for that price. I can't believe it, really. It is something I have always wanted."

In my mind, I am now thinking, "I thought Dave was a smart guy, a really good partner for me to be in business with. Now I really question his judgment. I don't even think we should be partners at all if he wants to set up shop in a junk pile full of dust and rodents." I say, "Gee, Dave, I completely disagree. In fact I am wondering if we should think of being in business together. I get the feeling that we just don't think alike."

Dave is now stunned. He thinks, "Gee, I thought Pat was a trustworthy, steady, kind person. Now I see that she is fickle and mean and totally unreliable." He says, "Maybe you are right." And there the partnership ends. Of course this is shortened in length for the sake of brevity, but things like this happen every day, don't they?

A Quiet Moment on the Bay

The movement between ego and spirit—or, as some authors call it, "brain" and "heart"—is a constant choice on a moment-by-moment basis. The religions of the world, and now, more recently psychological theories based on the mind/body movement, say that we need to train ourselves to live from the heart. We need to constantly remind ourselves that we always have a choice to act from the perspective of virtue or from the perspective of selfishness. We always have a choice to focus our attention on the wisdom of our hearts or to attend to the nervous chatter and static of our running thoughts. But as the following story will illustrate, belief, intention, attention, and action can interact in interesting ways that can fool us, deceive us, and keep us captive in lower states of consciousness. I will give you an example.

One beautiful fall day, my husband and I were on our boat in the Chesapeake Bay, anchored in a quiet lagoon. I had planned to use the time for some quiet prayer and meditation. In the words of our discussion here, my intention, or the choice of my heart, was to pray. I had been too busy lately and felt sort of out of balance. I was looking forward to some quiet time to calm down and get more in touch with my inner heart and sense of spiritual awareness.

Lots of other sailboats were also anchored there on this beautiful, warm, sunny day. As the sun began to set, my husband and I prepared for our favorite time of day. Traditionally, we make a simple supper and as we eat and watch the sunset, the peace and beauty of the surroundings and the gentle rocking motion of the boat lull us into an irresistible peace and restful state of mind. On this evening, the sunset was particularly spectacular, a blazing pink sky that gave the shimmering water a warm shade like pale pink roses. I relaxed and breathed, and in my heart I quietly thanked God for all the beauty around me. Just as I was getting into a feeling of blissful peace, an unbelievably loud noise blasted through the air. It sounded exactly—I mean exactly—like a jackhammer, and it was coming from a boat about fifty feet away! It appeared as if the people on an adjacent sailboat had begun running an electric generator. It was a big boat, and fancy too. It looked as if it had probably cost more than my house. "Rich people," I fumed to myself. My body tensed as if I had been shot. I began to stiffen and quiver. I was furious. My thoughts began racing with a story.

"How can people be so thoughtless? Look at them there, reading the newspaper while the rest of us can hardly think! What egotists! What selfish . . !" I am sure you can fill in the rest. I don't want to infect your mind with more of this kind of thinking.

Now let's take a look at this scenario and slow it down. Didn't I just say that my intention, my plan, or my choice had been to come to the bay to deepen myself spiritually? So what was I doing now?

Well, I can tell you what I was thinking, and you decide. I was thinking, "I would like to go over there and give them a piece of my mind—tell them off!" I could see myself in my mind's eye doing that, and then I could see the people on the other boat smirking back at me, with their Nautica togs, their martinis and their overly white teeth, shrugging and saying, "It's a free country, Madam. If you don't like it, there is a big bay out there."

"People like that," I thought, "just have no business being out here in nature when people like me—sensitive, caring, praying-type people—are trying to *commune* with *God*, for heaven's sake!"

Perhaps it was the rocking of the boat—I don't know—but just then I drifted off into a daydream for a few minutes. In my reverie, I became a ghost and could transport myself to the rich people's boat. I overheard the conversation of a man and a woman who were very, very old.

"Marvin, do we really need that generator? I can just imagine what all those young people think out there. We sound like we are jackhammering our boat."

"Margaret, you know I need the respirator, and the batteries on the boat only go so long. Every twelve hours we have to recharge or else we have to go home. That oxygen won't just jump out of those canisters on board. We decided 8 PM and 8 AM would be the least disturbing times and that an hour and half would be the shortest time possible. Everyone seems to be up and either having dinner or swimming. I am sure it will be OK."

Margaret quietly nodded and inside herself remembered (despite her *own* stories that were running), "This trip was Marvin's dying wish, and I have to cherish these last few months together. All those other people out there have the rest of their lives to see quiet sunsets."

My ghost self hung its head.

With this my reverie ended, and I looked over at the perfectly appointed boat next to me. Of course it was decked out with all the trimmings, this could be their last vacation together. How could I be so selfish, judging them that way?

In psychology, the kind of thinking I was doing before my daydream is called "projection." For some reason my husband calls the same thing, "transferal." He says we "transfer" the stories in our head out to other people and we make those stories belong to them. In other words, I projected or transferred my selfishness onto "the rich people" on the boat with the generator. It was I who was being egotistical and selfish, now, wasn't it? And I was making up a story to cover up this inner reality. I was "projecting" or transferring what was inside me to the outside.

Now, I have told this story many times to audiences. Often they say, "Don't be so hard on yourself, Pat. Those folks were making a lot of noise." They reason that my response was at least somewhat justified.

It is kind of them to say so, but remember my intention. My intention, the wish and the desire of my heart, was to come to the bay to progress spiritually. Let's take a closer look at that for a minute.

Living in Fiction

I will be honest with you. This story is true except for the daydream. I did indeed spend time on the bay and did encounter a boat that sounded like a jackhammer and did experience angry thoughts toward the people on the other boat. I also did make up fiction about what kind of people I thought they were. I did not actually fall into a reverie and find out I was all wrong. But the point is that I *could have.* I was, after all, *making things up.* I was creating a story and acting, feeling, and believing that my made-up story was true. I was living in fiction.

My husband, who is more kindhearted than I, also lives in fiction, but his kind heart makes up lovely stories about people to justify their unkind actions. If he sees a woman at 5:00 PM being rude to a sales clerk, he says, "These poor mothers who have to work full time and then go home and cook, too. No wonder they feel at the end of their ropes sometimes." He is making this fiction up, of course. He doesn't know the woman is a mother or that she even has a job. Or, if someone would dash in front of him and steal a parking place he was heading into, he would say something like, "Boy, I would hate to carry all the burdens that guy carries to be so stressed and in a hurry like he is." This is more fiction.

I, of course, being the psychologist that I am, occasionally tell my husband that he has to get with it. I tell him he has to stop "looking at the world through rose-colored glasses," that he is "in denial," and that he needs to "get real." Now my real face, instead of my ghost face, is hanging its head. At least his fiction is compassionate.

If you are going to make up fiction, why not make up fiction that at least keeps your heart attuned to compassion? If you are going to be crazy, you might as well be *kind* and crazy, instead of just crazy!

But now that I am studying and practicing about creating a spiritual reality, I see that there are better and much more productive ways to handle life than by creating fiction, compassionate or not. Let's keep the same example going and take a look at two more possible reactions to the loud boat scenario. I have been explaining that belief, attention, and intention interact with choices and create reality. Let's take a look at the boat story again and consider whether I really "missed the boat." Let's contrast my unexamined way of relating to the noise with a way of looking at it that is more in keeping with the process of inner awareness I am suggesting we try to cultivate. We have been saying that I always have a choice of at least two modes—one that is selfish and one that is not.

Old Way of Experiencing the Noise	New Way
Belief: I have the right to silence on the bay.	*Belief:* I am a servant to all. If those people need loud noises for some reason, then that is more important than my momentary comfort.
Attention: I feel angry and I am aware of that.	*Attention:* I thank them for giving me the opportunity to practice my spiritual discipline
Intention: I would like to make them uncomfortable and yell at them or shame them in some way so they will stop making this noise and apologize to me. My intention is to hurt them—to cause suffering to them.	*Intention:* I love them. I want them to be happy, even if that includes loud noise and whatever the loud noise provides. My intention is to love them more than myself.
Action: If the dinghy had the motor on it, I would at least go yell at them.	*Action:* I will wait a while and send loving thoughts to them. If the sound disturbs our sleep, we can move farther up the bay.

Tests to Help Us Grow

When my husband and I set sail on the bay, the deepest intention of my heart was to use the experience to pray and meditate. I wanted to feel closer to God. If I had been able to keep my focus on my intention and concentrate when I heard the noise, things might have gone something like this:

When I hear the noise like a jackhammer coming from the adjacent well-appointed boat, my *belief* is that "I want to strengthen myself spiritually. I know that while I'm living on this plane of existence, if I'm going to reach a level of union with God, I have to rid myself of the veils that separate me from the knowledge and experience of God. That means I need tests, and I need to practice passing those tests in order to advance. I welcome tests."

Perhaps at this point I notice the sound of the loud noise in my ears. I register the noise and begin to notice a feeling of alarm arising inside me. I stop what I am doing and focus inwardly on my inner experience. I focus on my breathing as I do this. My *attention* is on what is happening to me as I hear the jackhammer noise. I try to simply notice.

My *intention* is to advance myself spiritually and not contribute any negative thoughts, words, or deeds to the planet. I would like to emanate love. I choose to emanate love over the distraction of this noise. I remind myself that "it is just a noise." However, since I notice that it takes my concentration and attention to focus on love with this noise going on, I realize that this is a good opportunity for spiritual practice. I welcome it in my heart. In fact, I feel grateful for this chance to practice what I am now trying to learn.

I begin to notice that this loud noise really tries my patience, showing me that I need practice with patience. The *action* I take is to focus on my breathing and on feeling patience in my heart. I am grateful to these people who have put this loud noise in this unexpected spot when my intention in coming here was to pray.

Mindfulness

Notice that I just *noticed* the noise on the bay, but I did not react emotionally to it. Learning to just notice our outer experiences while keeping a focus on a clear spiritual intention and inner experience is called "mindfulness training" by many of the professionals associated with the Mind and Life organization I mentioned earlier. Jon Kabat-Zinn, Zindel Segal, and many others have developed structured protocols to teach people how to focus the mind and heart on inner reality. Mindfulness training is now widely used in hospitals and clinics as a treatment for anxiety and depression, and it has also been found useful in medicine, personal growth, sports, parenting, human relations, and many other disciplines. Studies confirm its effectiveness. The essence of mindfulness training is a focus of attention on the present moment and allowing it to "just be" as it is. While outer reality is flowing by, the focus of attention remains on inner reality, on the flow of the breath going in and out, on the feelings of the body as they experience sensations, on the constantly changing flow of emotion. Practitioners learn to distinguish between what is "inner" and what is "outer." They learn to make a clear distinction between things they can change (their beliefs, their attention, their intentions, their emotional responses) and things they perhaps cannot change (such as the noise on the bay).

Science and the Mind

If we were to have a scientist on board our boat, he/she could use a machine to measure the amplitude of the generator noise. He/she could tell us that the noise is 85 decibels, perhaps. Then the scientist could measure my heart rate and my blood pressure and things like that before and after the noise to see if the noise seemed to be correlated with a change in my physical body state as measured from the outside by the machinery of the scientist. But no matter how sophisticated the machinery, the scientist could only tell me things about what is going on *outside* myself. The scientist cannot tell from the outside precisely what is going on *inside* me. In other words, the scientist does not know how to access my experience of the sound. Only I can do that, and the process I must use is introspection, or looking inside.

Machines cannot explain or measure consciousness. Only introspection can shed light on your own consciousness. Only you can examine your own beliefs and how they influence your perceptions. Only you know what the true intentions of your heart really are. Only you can make a choice to pay attention to spiritual advancement, truth, and virtue, or to pursue self-interest, passion, or even evil.

My belief is that the task of my life is to find the blessings in everything. My job, therefore, is to be alert to my beliefs and to choose to be constantly aware that I am here to learn spiritual lessons. An ongoing spiritual lesson is the process of removing my own distortions of reality—distortions I am calling "stories" or "fiction"—and to live in spiritual reality. This is not a black and white, either/or, quick-fix kind of process. It is a process that develops over time with practice.

The Bahá'ís call the delusions we have, or the stories we make up, "veils" that separate us from our true spiritual nature. In the prayers that Bahá'ís say, they continuously ask God to remove these veils, because they understand that spiritual tests are presented to us to help burn away the veils that separate us from God. The tests are meant to give us an opportunity to grow in awareness and to advance spiritually.

The Bahá'í Faith also emphasizes the crucial importance of practicing meditation but does not specify a specific way or school of practice. Consider the following quotation from 'Abdu'l-Bahá:

> You cannot apply the name "man" to any being void of this faculty of meditation; without it he would be a mere animal, lower than the beasts. . . .
>
> The spirit of man is itself informed and strengthened during meditation; through it affairs of which man knew nothing are unfolded before his view. Through it he receives Divine inspiration, through it he receives heavenly food.
>
> Meditation is the key for opening the doors of mysteries. In that state man abstracts himself: in that state man withdraws himself from all outside objects; in that subjective mood he is immersed in the ocean of spiritual life and can unfold the secrets

of things-in-themselves. To illustrate this, think of man as endowed with two kinds of sight; when the power of insight is being used the outward power of vision does not see.

This faculty of meditation frees man from the animal nature, discerns the reality of things, puts man in touch with God.

This faculty brings forth from the invisible plane the sciences and arts. Through the meditative faculty inventions are made possible, colossal undertakings are carried out; through it governments can run smoothly. Through this faculty man enters into the very Kingdom of God.

Nevertheless some thoughts are useless to man; they are like waves moving in the sea without result. But if the faculty of meditation is bathed in the inner light and characterized with divine attributes, the results will be confirmed.

The meditative faculty is akin to the mirror; if you put it before earthly objects it will reflect them. Therefore if the spirit of man is contemplating earthly subjects he will be informed of these.

But if you turn the mirror of your spirits heavenwards, the heavenly constellations and the rays of the Sun of Reality will be reflected in your hearts, and the virtues of the Kingdom will be obtained.

Therefore let us keep this faculty rightly directed—turning it to the heavenly Sun and not to earthly objects—so that we may discover the secrets of the Kingdom, and comprehend the allegories of the Bible and the mysteries of the spirit.

May we indeed become mirrors reflecting the heavenly realities, and may we become so pure as to reflect the stars of heaven.[4]

Notice that 'Abdu'l-Bahá mentions the same choice I spoke of earlier, the choice of reflecting "heavenly realities" or the choice of reflecting "earthly objects." And notice, too, this idea that you can't do two things at once. You can't pay attention to outside things and inside things at the same time. He says when the power of insight is being used, "the outward power of vision does not see." Think of the Christian tradition of closing the eyes and bowing the head to pray. This action closes off the sense of sight, making it easier to access your inner wisdom, your inner senses.

Mindfulness meditation, which has its roots in the Buddhist traditions, is just one of many potentially helpful ways to slow down and take a look inside. Techniques from Eastern traditions include movement meditative techniques that engage the body in the inner focus work. Yoga, Tai Chi, and Qigong are a few of these methods. Any method or technique that helps you to slow down, calm down, and begin to develop an awareness of your inner core of peace and compassion is probably a good thing.

In the journal entries that follow, you will see me beginning my own spiritual journey, and you will see that I am beginning at square one. I have trouble with every aspect of spiritual development. In fact, I have trouble just sitting still! I have trouble believing strongly in the importance of this spiritual work. I have trouble focusing my attention. I often make the wrong choices and take the wrong actions. Still, I am trying. I am trying to become enlightened, and I have now become very committed to the process. Writing this book has brought me amazing spiritual benefits as the process itself has helped me to focus and really try to go deeper. The personal fruits of this labor, I promise you, are already more than worth the effort.

For my own spiritual journey, I have chosen to use prayer and meditation on sacred scripture as a method to advance. I have chosen the Seven Valleys because it is a description of stages of spiritual development. It describes the experiences one has within the different stages and helps guide one from one stage to the next.

In the past, I had read the Seven Valleys many times. I had found it pretty much inscrutable. But when I began to study it as part of the research for the first draft of this book, I found that even though I was not able to comprehend as much of it as I would like, I was nevertheless having some very surprising emotional experiences every time I studied it. Each time I studied the Seven Valleys I felt an inexplicable happiness deep in my heart. At first I thought I was simply having hormonal fluctuations. Then I wondered if the brand of tea I was drinking during my reading was particularly beneficial. Ah, the fiction I can spin! Finally, I began to realize that there was something more to it. As you will see from my first journal entries, I became more and more fascinated with the text over time—so much so that I eventually begin to describe my relationship to it as spiritually "addictive." I hope you will also find it interesting and inspiring. But remember, you can use this same type of process with *any* of the sacred scriptures from *any* of the spiritual traditions.

My own journaling began with a study of some short passages within the Seven Valleys text. I would choose a section and then copy the passage of text into my journal. Then I would meditate on the passage and just write whatever came into my awareness.

As you will see in my journal entries, I have been amazed at what has unfolded within my life as a result of this simple process. Once again, let me emphasize that it is the process I am "selling," not my own personal outcome. I invite you to experiment for yourself. I hope my text will inspire you to begin and stay with the process. As the chapters unfold and I consider one or another aspect of spiritual development, I will present some questions you can ask yourself to help "prime the pump." I am hoping that you will start your own spiritual journal and record some of your own insights. I am hoping you may want to share parts of your process with others. I am hoping that this book and your own journaling may provide the occasion for conversations about spiritual development with your friends and family. I am hoping this process will open channels of communication about spiritual issues among diverse groups of people, especially among those of different religious backgrounds.

So here we go. Grab a notebook and a pen. To find the complete text of the Seven Valleys, see the appendix. Keep these questions in mind as you go: What is your belief? What is your intention, and what choices are you making? What is your attention focused on? What actions are flowing from your inner belief system into the outer world?

The Seven Valleys as a Guide to Spiritual Development

The Seven Valleys was written by Bahá'u'lláh, during the period of his life in which he was in exile in Baghdad (1853–63). It is considered his "greatest mystical composition."[1] Much of the text of that composition will be included in the pages that follow, but the passages are not necessarily presented in their original order. While reading these meanderings of mine, you may wish to refer to the full text of the Seven Valleys in the appendix. Then you can more fully experience the spiritual power of the original text.

I chose to use the Seven Valleys as a guide and a vehicle for spiritual development because it reflects essential spiritual principles that are common to all the established religions. These principles are applicable to everyone because they reflect basic spiritual truths and realities. I became enthralled with the Seven Valleys after I had been reading extensively in the area of spiritual development across many disciplines and spiritual traditions. I found that sometimes, what it took an author a whole book to express, the Seven Valleys might express in one sentence or a short phrase.

Certainly, this distillation of truth into such a concise and powerful form makes the book uniquely powerful. It also makes it rather hard to understand.

I don't think you will find it easy to read the Seven Valleys straight through as you might a textbook or a novel. I think when you do that, you may come away perhaps confused or overwhelmed. The structure and poetic nature of the composition requires meditation. For this reason, to my mind, it is more akin to poetry than to prose.

You will notice that I do structure my journal entries in the order of stages that correspond to the sequence of seven valleys. But you will also notice that I pick and choose within those valleys the passages that spoke especially clearly to my heart. I had no plan or particular purpose in making the choices I did. I followed the promptings of my heart. I did find that doing it this way made the text of the Seven Valleys more understandable to me.

The idea of spiritual development is not new, nor does it uniquely belong to Bahá'u'lláh. Bahá'u'lláh wrote another similar letter on spiritual development called the Four Valleys. The stages are delineated for the sake of understanding. Much overlap and interweave among the stages and valleys is taken for granted. I am not describing a linear progression so much as an organic evolution of consciousness.

The reason for the number seven is unknown. Bahá'u'lláh wrote the Seven Valleys in the form of a letter to a friend. He explains that he is writing this letter to help his friend grow nearer to God. This is the way he puts it:

I therefore reveal unto thee sacred and resplendent tokens from the planes of glory, to attract thee into the court of holiness and nearness and beauty, and draw thee to a station wherein thou shalt see nothing in creation save the Face of thy Beloved One, the Honored, and behold all created things only as in the day wherein none hath a mention. . . .

. . . "And there shall appear upon the tablet of thine heart a writing of the subtle mysteries of 'Fear God and God will give you knowledge.'" 2

In days gone by, within other revelations of God such as Christianity, for instance, the deeper planes of spiritual knowledge were considered too difficult for the average citizen to strive for. Monks, nuns, and those devoted exclusively to spiritual striving sought mystic knowledge and lived their lives around this quest. Now the Bahá'í Faith calls everyone to strive to achieve this depth of knowledge. The Bahá'í Faith does not have any clergy. Every member of the religion is called to the deepest level of spiritual knowledge and service. All are called to know God at the deepest level possible and to apply this knowledge in the practical affairs of everyday life.

In the journal entries that follow, you will find the musings of one wanderer on the journey to the heavenly homeland. That wanderer, of course, is me. Remember that I am wandering. Don't follow me. Follow the compass of your own heart. You are free to find my wandering amusing as I make my primitive attempts to walk the Valleys. This journey is what I believe life is really about, but how often I lose that focus! It is amazing how easy it is to become distracted and how much the glitter of people and things can pull my attention away from my inner awareness. To keep myself attuned inwardly to that which is spiritual is my quest—the quest that I ask you, the reader, to join.

We must walk the spiritual path with practical feet. Only you can find your own spiritual path and determine how to apply your inner knowledge to the material world. Trust yourself, and trust the process. Here we go. Bahá'u'lláh describes the map of the territory we will travel in this way:

> . . . *The stages that mark the wayfarer's journey from the abode of dust to the heavenly homeland are said to be seven. Some have called these Seven Valleys, and others, Seven Cities. And they say that until the wayfarer taketh leave of self, and traverseth these stages, he shall never reach to the ocean of nearness and union, nor drink of the peerless wine. The first is the Valley of Search.*[3]

PART TWO

Seven Stages of
Spiritual Development

Stage One: The Valley of Search

"In Our ways will We guide them."
—BAHÁ'U'LLÁH, *THE SEVEN VALLEYS*

The journey of finding your true self, the self that is your spiritual core, is a journey that does not end. It begins in this physical life and continues into the life hereafter, through what Bahá'ís call "all the worlds of God," as your soul continually advances closer and closer to the presence of God. Within this earthly life, understood as the bottom-most rung of the spiritual ladder, your spiritual calling is to go inward and find this core and live from this core even within this material world. Material existence itself is but a mirage, an illusion, compared to the true reality of the soul.

Many of us, including myself, have not reached the higher stages of mystic knowing where these facts seem self-evidently true each day. If I were to reach that state of mystic knowing, I would live in a state of true and lasting happiness, contentment, and wonderment every moment of the day. Instead, as you will read in my journal entries, I am easily distracted with myriad material concerns and all sorts of thoughts and assumptions—you name it. These distractions take me away from my center of spiritual happiness, my true spiritual home.

In my journal entries, I trace some of my steps inward on the way to my spiritual enlightenment. You will see that I am limited by my own level of spiritual capacity and by the amount of time and effort I spend on my spiritual development. Nevertheless, I am finding the journey to be so valuable that I want to share it, humble though it may be.

The Seven Valleys will be my guide during this inward journey. It is a mystic text, meaning that it describes the process of the soul in language that the reasoning mind and senses can understand, but at the same time, the mere process of reading the text quickens the soul, too. Reading it and meditating upon it can begin to open you up to your own spiritual potential.

The best way to use this book is to read the passages from the Seven Valleys first and try to meditate upon them. Then, if you find it helpful to do so, read my journal entries, which convey the struggle I am making to move out of my material way of living and understanding toward a more spiritual way of understanding life.

It might also be helpful to begin your own spiritual journal, if you wish. My journal entries may suggest a possible model, but the most important thing is to follow the promptings of your own heart and soul. The questions within each section of this book may help you focus your attention on the text and on some of the key elements of moving inward.

Journal Entry 1: The Journey Inward Begins

> *Yea, these mentionings that have been made of the grades of knowledge relate to the knowledge of the Manifestations of that Sun of Reality, which casteth Its light upon the Mirrors. And the splendor of that light is in the hearts, yet it is hidden under the veilings of sense and the conditions of this earth, even as a candle within a lantern of iron, and only when the lantern is removed doth the light of the candle shine out.[1]*

I have been studying the Seven Valleys now for more than six months. Whenever someone asks me what I am working on, I tell them that I am "obsessed" with the Seven Valleys. I discovered it as I was preparing a book on the heart as a focal point of spiritual energy and guidance, and I noticed how often the heart is mentioned in the Seven Valleys. In the previous passage, Bahá'u'lláh tells me that the splendor of the light of his revelation is hidden in my own heart. In another Bahá'í text, 'Abdu'l-Bahá speaks of the "secret treasure" and of the "resplendent powers long hidden in human hearts."[2] I started looking through the text of the Seven Valleys and underlining the word "heart" every time it occurred. This process brought me into an intimate involvement with the text, and I found that the more time I spent focusing on it, the more I found myself going into a deep, peaceful, meditative state of mind as a result of my study. This state of mind was so wonderful that I began to truly understand those mystics who abandon all contact with the everyday world and seek only the deep, wordless, silent communion with God.

I have always been drawn to contemplation. Many years ago when I was a young mother, I would visit the Abbey of Gethsemani, where the famous Catholic monk Thomas Merton lived. It is in rural Kentucky, and I lived only a few hours from there. When I found myself needing a spiritual boost, I would drive there and just walk around the beautiful grounds. I would see the monks there silently, peacefully pursuing their lives of balance—prayer, work, rest, all ideally in balance.

My more recent plunge into the Seven Valleys has made me powerfully aware of how out of balance my own life has become. Instead of maintaining a balance of one-third prayer, one-third work, and one-third sleep, I think I am achieving something closer to two-thirds work, one-third sleep, and a dashed off prayer stuck in here and there like a sprig of parsley on a turkey dinner. Prayer has become dispensable, just a garnish, certainly not the main meal.

Bahá'u'lláh's words tell me that when I make my prayer life just a sprig, I live most of my life in the sensory world of this earth—a world he calls a veil—in other words, an illusion. Buddhism refers to the sensory world as a world of illusion and delusion also. For a Buddhist, sanity is spiritual enlightenment. Enlightenment is a state of full spiritual awareness, a state of being without the veils of the sensory world. Bahá'u'lláh says that when we are enlightened, our heart's light shines out like a bright sun. He likens the sensory world to a big slab of iron that blocks out the light of truth. Buddhists say that those of us who live in this kind of spiritual darkness of sensory experience are insane! We go about our lives thinking and behaving according to a whole set of beliefs and assumptions that are false. We live in a false reality.

So I begin this journey knowing three things. First, I know I should not trust my sensory experience. Second, I am aware that I do trust it, often more than I trust my own heart, so therefore, spiritually speaking, I am insane. Third, I have already experienced what Bahá'u'lláh tells me is true. He can guide me through these Valleys. He can get me out of here, out of the illusion and delusion of the material world and into true reality.

Questions: Beginning the Inward Journey

Think about the following questions. If you find it helpful, you may wish to write your responses to them in a journal.

1. Are you aware that within you, at the core of your being, you are light and spirit?
2. Does your daily experience include feeling the spiritual joy and happiness of your true nature?
3. If the answer is yes, how have you trained yourself not to rely on sensory experience to find spiritual truth?
4. If the answer is no, are you willing to consider learning how to achieve a state of mind in which you feel enlightenment, happiness, and compassion for others?
5. Think of some times during which your senses fooled you. What was that like?

6. Think of some times you listened to your heart. What was that like?

7. Think of some times when your heart and mind—that is, your spiritual intuition and your rational reasoning powers—were working together in harmony. What was that like?

Journal Entry 2: Attention

> *And the splendor of that light is in the hearts, yet it is hidden under the veilings of sense and the conditions of this earth, even as a candle within a lantern of iron, and only when the lantern is removed doth the light of the candle shine out.*[3]

This morning I awoke with a sense of peace and gratitude. I saw my journal and my fountain pen lying next to the bed on my night table. In my heart I could feel a sense of being on track and a vague longing to return to my writing.

Then my husband came upstairs with a pot of tea, two mugs, and the Saturday advertisements for a television set. We sipped tea and compared the prices of new high-definition television sets. Then I called my girlfriend on my cell phone to make plans to go shopping later in the day. Then my husband and I ate breakfast—oatmeal and raisins (it never goes out of style). He went outdoors to do chores. I ran upstairs seeking my journal and my prayer book, but then, I don't even quite remember how the train of thought unfolded, I found myself vacuuming! I *hate* to vacuum. As I scraped the brush along the floor, I heard my inner voice saying, "Don't trust sensory experience." And then I would see one more speck of dust, and now two, and now that rug near the dog's door—that is always a spot that really needs vacuuming.

Tuning in more carefully to what was happening inside me, it was very clear that I wanted to keep moving, keep seeing, hearing, tasting, touching, even if it was dust and dirt. I could feel my attention being drawn to the carpets. I felt pulled along by the very act of physically moving. "I'll pray later," I said to myself. "Maybe before bed, when I feel more like sitting still." Then I could see myself in my mind's eye, night after night, mumbling a two-line prayer and switching off the lamp all in one gesture, just as sleep envelopes me like a warm, comforting blanket of unconsciousness. I love to sleep. Busy, busy, busy, drop into sleep. Go, go, go, then unconscious.

So when am I truly conscious in that spiritual way I spoke of yesterday? When am I "sane"? When do I make time for inner reality? How can I get my attention to stop running me from this, to that, to this? I am thinking of my kids when they were about two years old. If they got into mischief, one of the ways to stop them was to distract them. "No, Honey, we don't play in the dirt in the flower pots. Here, have this color-ful play dough instead. Here, feel it, it squishes like this." And soon my little one's chubby hands would be as busy with the play dough as they had been with the dirt. Obviously, I have about as much control over my attention as a two year old does.

I am wondering now how I manage my own attention. Do I run it, or does it run me? I am seeing myself today avoiding my spiritual journal by focusing on the vacuuming and I hear the tape I play inside my head that goes with this choice. "These floors really are dirty and you really *need* to do this now, not later. Later you are going shopping and then you'll forget or you won't feel like it."

I am already bored hearing the drone of the voice in my own head. I can still feel my heart longing to go to a quiet place and a quiet state of mind, but I just can't seem to stop my body from moving and my brain from running like a radio station stuck on a talk show channel.

Questions: Attention

Think of attention as being like a flashlight beam in a dark room. Wherever you shine the light, the objects in the room become visible. You cannot be aware of something you are not attending to. Attention is your flashlight. You shine your attention on something and then you perceive it. Attention is within your control.

1. What do you pay attention to? Make a graph or a list. How much time do you devote to developing your inner awareness versus the time you spend being aware of sensory experience and material reality?

2.   Do you consciously choose to pay attention to certain things and not other things? In other words, are you running your attention or is your attention running you?

3.   What do you think of the Buddhist idea that being focused on outward material things and sensory experience and just letting attention wander wherever it goes is a form of insanity?

Meditation Exercise 1: The Relaxation Response

Herbert Benson is a pioneer in the Mind/Body Movement. His research on the beneficial effects of what he called "The Relaxation Response" date to the publication of a book by the same name in 1975. In 1979 he continued this work in *The Mind/Body Effect*. Then, Dr. Benson became interested in the impact of spiritual beliefs on the mind and the body. Through his research, he found that combining a prayerful attitude with a "relaxation exercise" yielded more positive results than just relaxing alone. In 1984 he published *Beyond the Relaxation Response* in which he explored what he called "The Faith Factor."

The following advice about meditation is based on *The Wellness Book: The Comprehensive Guide to Maintaining Health and Treating Stress-Related Illness*, (1992), by Dr. Benson and Eileen Stuart. The book is a valuable resource for a variety of practices to reduce stress and improve overall physical and mental health. I have been recommending it to people I work with for many years.

Dr. Benson's Mind/Body Medical Institute sponsors a yearly conference on Spirituality and Healing. You can find out more information at info@mbmi.org.

Dr. Benson's work shows that two basic elements are needed to elicit the relaxation response: first, you need to choose something on which to focus your attention while relaxing the muscles of your body, and secondly, you need to keep returning your attention to the chosen focus with a gentle, passive, forgiving attitude. That's it. It is as simple as that. Something on which to focus your attention could be as rudimentary as your breath. That is all you need to do, just breathe and pay attention to your breathing as you focus your attention inward. If your attention drifts, gently bring it back to the focus of your breath. This simple formula is a "basic" for all meditative practice.

Everyone's attention wanders, especially as they begin meditative practice. If you get discouraged and give up when this happens, no progress will be made. It is important to have patience with yourself. When the inevitable drift of attention occurs, do not become upset with yourself or chide yourself. Definitely don't let your mind wander off on its own either! No, gently and passively and compassionately bring your attention back, again and again, to your chosen focus and your breath.

Skill at controlling attention takes practice. It doesn't come easily at first. Many people have trouble focusing even for a minute or maybe less. But with practice, especially daily practice, your skills will build quickly and you will soon be reaping the rewards of meditation.

It is important that you tailor your meditation to what suits you the best. Pick something that you like. If you are "fidgety" and find it hard to sit still, perhaps you might want to choose a walking meditation. You would still be focused inwardly and aware of your breath. My local Buddhist organization offers "walking meditations" to the general public. Groups gather and walk in silence while meditating. You don't need a group to do it, though. You can do your own walking meditation by paying attention to your breath and then walking slowly and deliberately, noticing the placement of each step, feeling your feet on the ground as you breathe in concert with your steps. Do this for 20 or 30 minutes if you can. You might or might not want to choose a focus word to say inwardly with each step.

In Catholicism, sometimes the rosary is said in a walking meditation. The repetitive prayers coupled with the movement and inner focus can be a powerful meditative practice. At other times, Catholics pray the rosary privately or with others in a seated position. The rosary itself is a meditative practice.

While the simplest repetitive focus can have beneficial health effects, Dr. Benson's work has shown that combining your breath focus with the repetition of a word or phrase that is linked to your spiritual beliefs makes the experience even more powerful. Some people I have worked with have chosen a word to which they repeatedly meditate. Let us take for example the word "Love". Their daily practice combines the rhythmic, relaxing breathing and focus of attention on the word "love." Then, if they later find themselves in a stressful circumstance, they need only focus inwardly briefly, and repeat their word to elicit the relaxation response. Their word becomes an automatic cue to shift the mind/body out of a stress response into a "relaxation" response. Through this practice, you can become an expert in remaining calm and focused in almost any circumstance.

To begin:

1. Get in a comfortable relaxed position where you can be alone and focus for a period of time. (Don't do this while doing something else! I had some folks try to meditate while driving their car! Remember, you want an *inward* focus.)
2. Choose a word or short phrase on which to focus. If possible, choose a word that is associated with your spiritual pathway.
3. Close your eyes or focus inwardly with eyes open by shifting attention inward on your breath and on your word.
4. Breathe normally and evenly and as you exhale, repeat your chosen word or phrase.
5. Remember to retain a passive attitude and to return your attention to your breath and your word whenever your attention drifts.

Journal Entry 3: Balancing Head and Heart

> *Some hold to reason and deny whatever the reason comprehendeth*
> *not, and yet weak minds can never grasp the matters which we*
> *have related, but only the Supreme, Divine Intelligence can com-*
> *prehend them:*
>> *How can feeble reason encompass the Qur'án,*
>> *Or the spider snare a phoenix in her web?*[4]

I am aware of another passage in Bahá'u'lláh's writings that says, "Wouldst thou that the mind should not entrap thee? Teach it the science of the love of God!"[5] As I ponder these verses, it hits me right between the eyes that Bahá'u'lláh says we need to learn the *science* of the love of God so that our *mind* does not entrap us. In other words, we need to study the science of love systematically so that we can overcome our egotistical mind. These are the same basic ideas that Buddhism claims as its goal.

In December 2005 I attended an amazing conference. It was in Washington DC, in the hall of the Daughters of the American Revolution. Secret Service agents patrolled the premises and security was tight. Eminent scientists were gathered for a three-day conference with the Dalai Lama of Tibet! This was to be another in a yearly ongoing dialogue between them and His Holiness. Before this time, most of the dialogues had been closed to all but a very few select invitees, and for the most part, only those who participated in the discussions could be present. The results of the conferences were published in books. This year, though, the dialogue was taking place in a large convention hall so that people like me could attend. Neurologists, brain researchers, mental health practitioners, and meditation researchers were all present along with the Dalai Lama and a number of Tibetan monks. The goal of the dialogue was to gain knowledge by comparing points of similarity and difference between the knowledge embodied within Buddhism and that within Western mind-science—that is, psychology, psychiatry, neurology, and related fields. (www.mindandlife.org)

Buddhism—in this case, Tibetan Buddhism—does not consider itself so much a religion as a science of the mind. The Dalai Lama makes the point that he comes to this consultation to learn as much as to teach. He brings with him a cadre of orange-robed monks who all seem to gleam with an inner light. Bright and shining faces, they have, and they exude a quiet happiness, confidence, and humility. It is my reflexive response to think that I want to be like them. "I want what they have," I say to myself.

The scientists gather on the big stage under lights and recording devices that memorialize the meeting. Despite the setting, every effort is made to create a casual living-room atmosphere and feeling. All the scientists are seated in comfortable chairs around a coffee table. One by one they make their presentations. But instead of a big lectern, Powerpoint presentations, complex statistics, or graphs, there is instead a quiet conversation. Often the pace of the proceedings is slowed by the need to translate the concepts from English to the Tibeto-Burman language of the Dalai Lama or vice versa.

Because the pace is slow and the goal is to communicate concepts, not to bedazzle and outdo each other by running a mass of numbers past the audience, I understand what the scientists are saying. I can hear, and what I hear astounds me. I listen, and inside me I feel a strong sense of recognition. I recognize the information's core wisdom. I've learned these things already, many things at least, from the Bahá'í writings I have been studying.

The scientists are saying that they have searched and searched for a control center in the brain and they haven't found one. They say that the brain is organized like a big interconnected network that operates as a whole. One scientist uses a word that I keep mulling over and over in my mind. He says the brain is an oscillator. To oscillate is to move or to swing back and forth, like a pendulum on a clock. When you are oscillating you are in a constant state of motion and change. Scientific evidence is being accumulated from a variety of fields and sources showing that human beings are energy oscillators. Physically, we know that our breath oscillates; it goes in and out, in and out. We know our heart oscillates; it pumps blood in and out of the heart, forcing it through our blood vessels. If you think about it for a moment, your physical body is never totally at rest, totally without oscillating, back and forth movement. If your body reaches that state of total stillness, your physical body will be dead.

We know that life on the physical plane involves this movement, this rhythm, this beat. We know, too, that our emotional life and our sense of happiness and well-being are intimately tied into the idea of regulating the oscillating rhythms of life so that they are harmonious, balanced, and coherent. So if physically I am oscillating, in a state of constant movement in my mind/body/spirit, what does this feel like? How do mind and body and spirit balance this movement, this oscillation?

This question is very complex both scientifically and spiritually. It gets me thinking about myself as an oscillator—as one who swings back and forth between my spiritual, heart-centered intuition and my reasoning brain. This swinging, or in my case tugging and pulling action, was reflected in my conflict yesterday morning when my heart longed to pray, reflect, and write and instead I reasoned that I should vacuum. This is the conflict between "feeble reason" and the heart, between the ego and the spirit, between the material and the ineffable.

A friend of mine, Elena Mustakova-Possardt, wrote about this conflict in a book called *Critical Consciousness: A Study of Morality in Global Historical Context.* She begins the book by saying,

> *The task I face feels overwhelming, and at the same time lucid and simple, a perfect example of the split between mind and heart with which most of us struggle: the heart knows, and the mind has to figure out. Each has its tasks and its powers, and*

*in synergy they are an undefeated team. Yet, it is so easy to be-
come frightened, and then the mind begins to spin its wheels,
taking us further and further away from the inner vision of the
heart.[6]*

The spirit of Elena's words echoed constantly throughout
the DAR convention center last winter. From my perspective
it seemed like a showdown—*reason* on this side of the ring,
represented by Western neuroscience and psychiatry, and
heart on the opposite side of the ring, represented by two
thousand years of Buddhist tradition. Reason boasts of ob-
jectivity, statistics, and computerized images of the brain at
work. "Hard science," we call it. Somehow a puffed up chest,
a nose in the air, and a haughty tone always seem to associate themselves with these words—hard science, my friend,
very hard.

And on the other side of the ring sit the men in orange,
the mediators who claim *reason* is the enemy. Reason, they
claim, serves its master, the ego. The Dalai Lama, as a fol-
lower of the Buddha, works daily to defeat the ego so that
pure consciousness, enlightenment, may triumph. His science,
he says, smiling softly as he explains, is based on rigorous
methods that are systematic and thoroughly researched—
quite scientific. However, his method is introspective. Inner
reality is the landscape of interest. He seems almost puzzled
by what he sees as the illogical approach of trying to understand what goes on *inside* a human being's consciousness
and inner experience by looking *outside* that human being.

He is never haughty or puffed up—quite the opposite. He is truthful, though. He believes that the keys to wisdom lie within, within the wisdom of the heart. He speaks softly, kindly, urging the cultivation of compassion to bring happiness to oneself, to others, and to the world.

As I write these words, two things begin to happen inside me. I feel myself calming and becoming more relaxed, more detached. I begin to feel that pull inward, and I begin to lose focus on the things around me in the room, I begin to let go of my mental to-do list. Suddenly, I am wrenched out of this drift inward by a loud inner thought that sends panic through my body: I don't know where my cell phone is! I jump up and go scurrying around looking for it, completely breaking my concentration and taking myself spinning out of that inward place I was drifting toward. I grab the home phone and dial my cell phone! Ring, ring . . . I hear it! And then awareness quietly nudges me. "Hello, Pat, you are calling yourself from one machine in order to reach another machine!" I lower my head with an inner embarrassment. Let's see, how long was that meditation? I don't think I got up to ten seconds! Uh, maybe it was two seconds. Maybe just the thought of going inward at all scares the dickens out of me and I just panic and grab for the familiar—something outside, a machine, yeah, a machine. We Westerners love machines!

As I scurry and think of writing about this ridiculous experience, I am aware that this is actually what I do. I am not making this up to make a good story. This is me. I am afraid to go inward for fear of what I will find there.

Questions: Balance between Head and Heart

1. I speak of two ways of knowing, one based on the "head" and the other on the "heart." While I am attracted to the heart-based, non-sensory way of knowing, I also constantly avoid it and concentrate on material concerns. Does this ever happen to you? How do you overcome the pull of the material and stay focused on inner processes? Do you even think this is a good idea? If so, why? If not, why not?

2. Sometimes people are afraid to "go inside" because they fear what lies within. They may have feelings they do not wish to face, or they may have scars from previous life events or negative relationship experiences. How comfortable are you going inward?

3. What kind of information do you trust the most? Rank these ways of knowing, and explain why you trust this way of knowing more than other ways:

____ What I see and hear for myself
____ The results of well-conducted scientific studies
____ Advice from sacred writings and holy scriptures
____ Reasonable logical arguments
____ My own intuition
____ What others tell me
____ Tradition
____ Whatever I think based on my past experience
____ Other

Journal Entry 4: Fear

In their search, they . . . seek at every moment to journey from the plane of heedlessness into the realm of being. No bond shall hold them back, and no counsel shall deter them.[7]

Elena's statement sums it up so well for me: "It is so easy to become frightened, and then the mind begins to spin its wheels, taking us further and further away from the inner vision of the heart." The passage above from the Seven Valleys says, "No bond shall hold them back." Fear is the bond that holds me back. I am frightened of the power of my heart.

Six months ago when this journey through the Valleys began, I came to a sudden awareness that truth is available to me within the inner depths of my heart. I posed a question to my heart: Why, really, did my divorce occur seven years ago? I have always carried within me so many unanswered questions about it. I posed the question sincerely, confident that the answers would be presently revealed. Then, astoundingly, I refused to hear. I slammed closed the book of my heart along with all the copies of the Seven Valleys scattered about the house. I got "busy" and I got very scared. I could feel the emotional pressure of the information, and it felt like a huge dam was about to break inside me. I felt as if all that pent-up pressure was going to rush over me and knock me out cold, sweep me away.

It took many months of busyness and distraction, accompanied by an increasing sense of distress, before my now burdened ego was ready to surrender control. In a state of prayer, my answers came simply and made sense. But in all honesty, these answers had never occurred to my "reason." Once revealed, my ego's reasoning mind took days, weeks, and months, to really process what my heart had revealed in a few seconds. My heart had always known, had always held that information, and now, safe and sound in a new life, my reasoning mind was finally ready to deal with reality.

I am fond of describing my job as a psychologist who does psychotherapy this way: I tell people what they already know but don't want to hear, and I only know this truth because they just told me!

My clients come to me with their stories, and embedded within them I hear another story. I hear what their lips utter, but veiled beneath the utterance, the heart also speaks. Sometimes I can actually "hear" their heart by attuning my own heart to theirs. Truth, of course, is what I seek, and when those I work with hear their own truth put out there for eye and ear to see and hear, they are hit hard emotionally. This truth of the heart has been blocked from their reasoning mind. Now "feeble reason" must deal with it.

The session in which a moment like this occurs is transformative. I refer to it as *the* session. Before *the* session, I am listening and maybe working more on the surface levels. The relationship builds, and if *the* session is to occur, it is only after I have turned the matter over in my own heart and only after trust is strong and my intention to help is clear. Then I try to speak from my own heart to the heart of the other.

This is a risky moment, and some fear must be overcome in order to go forward. Our connection can be broken if my words land without a clear and sincere cushion of care and concern surrounding them—compassion, the Dalai Lama calls it.

My experiences in these moments of deep connection with others have shown me the power and beauty of heart-wisdom in action. I trust this process, and I trust my own heart's intuition when it comes to helping others. How interesting that I find myself afraid of applying this same confidence to my own inner process.

Questions: Fear

1. Do you ever feel afraid to face yourself? Do you sometimes avoid the truth of your own heart?
2. The journal entry talks about a conflict between wanting to know the truth and not wanting to face the truth. Do you ever feel this way, pulled in two directions? How do you handle this situation? How do you resolve the inner conflict?
3. The quote in this section says "it's so easy to become frightened." Some people live their life organized around fear, trying to avoid things that scare them, trying to numb out the anxiety with external things (drugs, alcohol, sex, food, money, power, and so on). Do you live fearlessly?

4. Identify the people, contexts, thoughts, feelings, ideas, situations, etc., that frighten you. When you get frightened inside, how do you react on the outside? What happens? What do you do?
5. When you feel frightened, how do you regain a sense of safety and comfort? Who or what do you turn to?
6. Do you know how to find comfort and safety within your own heart through meditation and prayer?

Meditation Exercise 2: A Safe Place

Review the meditation practices on page 72 in regard to preparation, focus, and breathing. To this meditation, you may add a visualization that will allow you to increase feelings of safety. While your eyes are closed and you are entering the meditative state, imagine yourself in a place that is perfect for you. Imagine the place, either real or imaginary, where you find the greatest comfort, peace, and security. Perhaps it is your own home, or a mountain, or a magic carpet. It doesn't matter what you choose. It only matters that the place is perfectly safe for you. When you decide on the place, picture yourself in that safe place. Fill in the details of the picture. Notice the sights, sounds, smells, textures, and so on. Stay in this place in your mind as you practice your breathing and your word from Exercise 1.

Journal Entry 5: Veils

> *In their search, they have stoutly girded up the loins of service, and seek at every moment to journey from the plane of heedlessness into the realm of being. No bond shall hold them back, and no counsel shall deter them.*[8]

Even my own feeble reason is now clear that, given my internal conflicts, my fears, my attachment to sensory experience and material things, and my lack of control over my own attention, I need help. There is no way to progress spiritually if I just keep doing what comes naturally. What comes naturally or automatically to me are the old habits of mind, which the passage just quoted calls "heedlessness." I repeat what I already know how to do and what I have done over and over again in the past. When I do that, especially when I do that without any awareness of what I am doing and why I am doing it, I act in a state of unconsciousness—a state of mind that Bahá'u'lláh calls "heedless." In other passages he calls this state "completely veiled."[9] None of the light of my soul—well, maybe a very small fraction of the light of my soul—ekes out through the layers upon layers upon layers of veils that lie between my understanding of what is going on and true spiritual reality.

I used to have a recurring dream about a car going down the road with no one at the steering wheel. The car was moving, but no one was driving it. There was plenty of action, noise, power—even the power to destroy—locked up in the engine of that car. It was a scary, eerie dream, and I always wondered what it meant. Now I think I am the car. It's my car, you know, and it's clear to me that sometimes no one is at the wheel. Sometimes I am sleeping at the wheel. But then there are those times, those precious times when I have traveled, ever so briefly, through paradise. And what do I remember?

Moments of exquisite happiness while being in a wheat field, just watching the wheat blowing in the wind. Or the night when I watched the fireflies blinking off and on, little pinpricks of light. As I watched them I wondered if that is what God sees when He looks down from heaven and sees the lights of our souls, now turned toward Him and burning brightly, now dark and turned away, and then, yes, a flicker again of light that quickly grows dark once again. A silly anthropomorphism of God, I know. And yet, that night, I seemed to see Creation not just with my outer eyes, but with my inner eyes as well. It was as if those fireflies were portals into the heart of creation. I could feel the heartbeat of the Creator in the pulse of His creation. My awareness lasted only briefly. And yet, all these many years later, my memory of it is as vivid as if it were yesterday.

Bahá'u'lláh tells us that we have available to us different planes or grades of consciousness. Other writers call these different levels of consciousness. In psychology and other academic disciplines there is a lot of talk about consciousness these days. The human potential movement, transpersonal psychology, spiritually oriented psychotherapy, new age spiritual movements, mindfulness-based practices based on Buddhist traditions—all of these focus on consciousness, how it arises, how we can become enlightened and raise our consciousness to greater levels of understanding.

In the Seven Valleys, Bahá'u'lláh gives me both the map and the vehicle to journey from lower states of mind to higher states. Just the reading and meditating I did, really more or less by accident while beginning the research on heart wisdom, began to palpably transform my awareness. Thus my newfound "addiction" to this text. He describes the territory I will pass through on my journey from what he calls "the abode of dust to the heavenly homeland."[10]

Questions: Veils

1. Bahá'u'lláh tells us that different states of consciousness are available to all of us. Some shifts in consciousness are unmistakable—sleep, being "drugged" or under the influence of alcohol, or the state we call "falling in love." Think about the different states of consciousness you have experienced. Have they been positive or negative?

2. Do you know how to exert control over your state of consciousness? Can you go into a state of deep mental peace and relaxation when you choose?

3. The Seven Valleys lead to what the text calls "our heavenly homeland." What do you think it would be like to

live in this heavenly homeland? Can you live there on a normal day-to-day basis? How would that state of mind be different than your usual day-to-day state of mind?

4. Can you think of friends or acquaintances who seem consistently to be in higher states of consciousness? How about lower states? Compare the characteristics of the higher and lower states.

Journal Entry 6: Patience

> *The steed of this Valley is patience; without patience the wayfarer on this journey will reach nowhere and attain no goal.*[11]

I am aware today that my journey thus far has mainly illumined the enormity of the task of overcoming my ego's nature. I am reminded of a comment my youngest son once made about a friend in the neighborhood who was backbiting about us and causing all sorts of pain and disruption. He said, "I am sure Mr. . . . has a good soul, Mom. It's what's wrapped around it that's the problem." My son was about six years old at the time. I have quoted him often.

I am sure my friend and I both have a good soul in there somewhere, but I am more and more aware of all the junk I have wrapped around mine. The Bible compares hiding the light of the soul under all these habits of mind and heart to putting a bushel basket over a candle.[12]

Questions: Patience

1. Where is your attention and energy focused? What are you earnestly striving for?
2. Do you ever feel conflicted about your striving? Does part of you want this and part of you want that? How do you decide what wins out?
3. Do you have patience with yourself? Are you compassionate toward yourself and your own limitations and problems?
4. Is it OK to try and fail?
5. Is it OK not to be perfect?
6. Is it OK to be wrong?
7. Is it OK to ask for help and guidance?
8. Is it OK to stop just going through the motions and "getting things done" and take time to stop, reflect, and allow your activity to flow from your inner convictions, your heart, your true self?

Journal Entry 7: Ardor

> *Nor should he ever be downhearted; if he strive for a hundred thousand years and yet fail to behold the beauty of the Friend, he should not falter.*[13]

A hundred thousand years! Wow, that sounds like something a little kid would say: "Mom, do you expect me to keep weeding this garden in this hot sun forever? I have been out here for a hundred thousand years!" I can hear myself as the mom answering back, chiming out through the screen door, "Keep at it, Honey. You'll get there."

I had to smile to myself when I read that Bahá'u'lláh says we have to measure progress in this Valley of Search "by the standard of the Majnún of Love."[14] *Majnún* means literally "insane." This is the title of the celebrated lover of ancient Persian and Arabian lore, whose beloved was Laylí, daughter of an Arabian prince. Symbolizing true human love bordering on the divine, the story has been the theme of many a Persian romantic poem.

Here we go with that insane idea again. I begin the journey insane and seeking sanity. In light of yesterday's fixation with vacuuming up the dust, I could hardly believe what the text says next:

> *It is related one day they came upon the Majnún sifting the dust, and his tears flowing down. They said, "What doest thou?" He said, "I seek for Laylí." They cried, "Alas for thee! Laylí is of pure spirit, and thou seekest her in the dust!" He said, "I seek her everywhere; haply somewhere I shall find her."*
>
> *Yea, although to the wise it be shameful to seek the Lord of Lords in the dust, yet this betokeneth intense ardor in searching. "Whoso seeketh out a thing with zeal shall find it."* [15]

I seek everywhere the quote says, everywhere, all the time, with intense ardor. I am looking up "ardor" in the dictionary.

I never use the word myself, and I seldom read it. It sounds like some vague out of fashion virtue that no longer concerns me, like chivalry. When I hear "chivalry" I envision a guy in a suit of armor like the knights of old would wear for jousting. I see him galloping on a horse, pointing a spear at some other equally chivalrous fellow coming at him on a different-colored horse. Chivalry is definitely out of style in my mind.

Ardor? "Ardor," *Webster's English Dictionary* says, comes from a French word for fire, and it means "1. fire, intense heat. . . ." It also means "2. emotional warmth or heat; eagerness; as, he pursues study with ardor; they fought with ardor. 3. bright spirit; brilliancy (obsolete)." The dictionary says synonyms include "devotion, earnestness, excitement, fervor, intensity, passion, rapture, zeal."

This is beginning to sound like it will require a lot of work. I feel like the kid pulling weeds in the garden. I am going to be sweating for a hundred thousand years here and never getting anywhere.

With that thought, my "meditation" ended and I got up to continue my spring cleaning. I knew those fireplace irons I tried to throw away three times were still sitting in the hallway. My husband said they were "antique brass" and "handy" when he builds a fire. "Don't throw them away," he said. To me, they just looked dirty and dingy and old, but I figured maybe if they were solid brass, I could shine them up.

As the phrase "intense ardor" kept rolling around in my mind, I grabbed the bottle of tarnish remover and poured it on the shovel of the fireplace set. After a few minutes of rubbing, the dirty, dull brown color gave way to a sparkle of the brass below the layers of tarnish. I rubbed, and even I could not miss the significance of my action. The more I rubbed away the tarnish, the brighter the brass shone. Inside, my heart continued to focus on the idea that I had to decide whether I was really up for this journey or not. Did I have the eagerness, the heat? "Maybe I am too old," I thought. "Maybe monks and people like that start out when they are young and eager"—more helpful thoughts from feeble reason. I kept polishing.

It started to be fun. The more I rubbed, the brighter the shine. Forget the fact that the set of tools doesn't look new or perfect. It looks better. "That's me," I said to myself. "All that tarnish covering up the gleam inside."

Then I hear reason chiming in. "This is hokey. It goes too well with what you are meditating about." I smile.

Feeble reason didn't *plan* my tarnish removal. I just started moving around while keeping my spiritual thoughts in mind. I began noticing that this cleaning feels so much different than the vacuuming that I did to hide or escape from my inner journey. Now my hands are moving, my body is doing its chores, and my spirit is engaged and learning symbolically from what I see with my physical eyes. My inner eyes are open and focused on this question: Can I find within myself the true, honest motivation and emotional energy—heat, ardor—to move forward?

My efforts gradually remove more layers of tarnish, and I feel, more than hear or think, the response to my question. "Just try. Even a little progress is better than no progress at all. Look at the fireplace shovel. It is pitted, it is still spotted with tarnish, but now it has a certain antique charm. Yeah, that's me—I have 'antique charm.' Because of the polishing, the fireplace set doesn't look like junk anymore. Maybe when you clean every few weeks you can shine the set a little more. Then it will get shinier instead of duller over time."

Questions: Ardor

1. Do you ever feel worthless, like the fireplace shovel, as if you were something that is a throwaway? How have your veils created this delusion? You have the same bright and shiny soul as everyone else on the planet. Is "feeble reason" rattling in your head? Do you have old emotional scars creating veils between you and your bliss?
2. With patience and ardor you can achieve your natural state of inner peace and happiness and maintain it. Are you willing to try?
3. What happens when you work hard for a while and fail to reach the goal? Do you become discouraged and give up? How can you plan for discouragement so you won't give up when this veil comes along?

Journal Entry 8: Aid from the Invisible Realm

> *In this journey the seeker reacheth a stage wherein he seeth all created things wandering distracted in search of the Friend. How many a Jacob will he see, hunting after his Joseph; he will behold many a lover, hasting to seek the Beloved, he will witness a world of desiring ones searching after the One Desired. At every moment he findeth a weighty matter, in every hour he becometh aware of a mystery; for he hath taken his heart away from both worlds, and set out for the Ka'bih of the Beloved. At every step, aid from the Invisible Realm will attend him and the heat of his search will grow.[16]*

I guess there is really nothing to feel frustrated or down-hearted about. Bahá'u'lláh says that my idea of "just trying" will definitely work. He seems to be saying that it was a good idea for me to be mindful of my spiritual question when I was polishing the fireplace irons. He says, "At every moment he findeth a weighty matter; in every hour he becometh aware of a mystery." I am finding it pretty amazing that I can actually follow this path and make some sense out of it, even in my ordinary, mundane life. I did get tickled when I connected the tarnish removal with removing the veils from my heart. I think that proves the next thing in the quote, "At every step, aid from the Invisible Realm will attend him." I am aware that setting my intention to grow spiritually and taking this action to concentrate and focus my attention on these matters seems to bring forth this aid and assistance. I feel that peace and calm come over me more and more now. I feel focused and happy, and I am more and more eager to progress and learn more. The text says it works that way. As the aid from the Invisible Realm assists me, "the heat of his search will grow." That is the ardor I was talking about before.

In this Valley of Search, as I am becoming more aware spiritually, I definitely see how much unhappiness in the world results from lack of spiritual awareness. People are searching for happiness in all the wrong places. Bahá'u'lláh says that we are all "distracted" by material concerns—jobs, money, "busyness," and we don't realize that the happiness we seek is just a step away, inside our own hearts.

Questions: *Aid from the Invisible Realm*

1. Where do you turn for help when you feel unhappy, stressed, frightened? Can you turn to receive help from the Invisible Realm?
2. What are your distractions? Are you addicted to something that you crave—food, sex, drugs, alcohol, attention, power, money, prestige, physical pleasures, proving your superiority, things like new cars, a big house? The list can go on and on.
3. Do you believe that you will receive aid from the Invisible Realm if you turn your attention to God? Do you think you can receive it even if you don't believe it is

possible? Do you think others receive this aid, but you can't or won't or don't?

4. What does this aid look like in your life? Do you think, "Everything happens for a reason"? Do you think there are spiritual lessons to be learned in even the most everyday affairs of life?

Journal Entry 9:
The Heart, a Wellspring of Divine Treasure

It is incumbent on these servants that they cleanse the heart, which is the wellspring of divine treasures—from every marking, and that they turn away from imitation, which is following the traces of their forefathers and sires, and shut the door of friendliness and enmity upon all the people of the earth.[17]

Even though this idea of cleansing came very early in the text, I kept avoiding it as I read the text again and again. Cleanse the heart. How to do that?

Many months ago I stumbled across some information about the actual physical heart that I found fascinating. The information came from a book by Joseph Chilton Pearce called *The Biology of Transcendence: A Blueprint of the Human Spirit.* Pearce's book includes a chapter called "The Triune Heart." He talks about the fact that the heart is much more than just a pump of blood. Pearce discusses other aspects of the heart that I had never heard about before I stumbled upon his book. It seems that the heart has at least three other functions I never understood. For one, it is a strong generator of electromagnetic energy. There is evidence that emotions like love and hate actually generate an electrical energy that travels and can be measured with electronic measuring devices! Secondly, the heart is a center of emotion because it has uninterrupted communication with the emotional centers of the brain. So feeling emotions in your heart is not just a metaphor. It is a physiological reality. And third, the heart has a kind of "brain" because the same neurotransmitters that function in the brain also function in the heart ganglia.

Increasingly, scientists and mental health parishioners are becoming interested in the role of the heart in experiencing and regulating human emotion. In the book, *The Instinct to Heal: Curing Stress, Anxiety, and Depression Without Drugs and Without Talk Therapy*, David Servan-Schreiber, MD, PH.D. Co-Founder of the Center for Complementary Medicine at the University of Pittsburgh Medical Center, discusses the heart's role in our everyday experiences. He says,"Clearly, the references to the heart in the words we use to describe our emotions are more than mere metaphors. It perceives and feels. It partly sets its own course of action. And when it expresses itself, it influences the physiology of our whole body, including the brain."[18]

Dr. Servan-Schreiber explains how that occurs. He explains that the human autonomic nervous system (ANS) regulates all the unconscious and life-giving systems within the human body. Your breathing, your kidney function, your heart beating, sweating, all these things and more are regulated by the ANS. The ANS is divided into two parts, the sympathetic system and the parasympathetic system. Dr. Servan-Schreiber calls the sympathetic system the "accelerator" and the parasympathetic system the "brakes." He explains that when your body needs to "rev up," when you are under attack (or falling in love!), your adrenaline kicks in, your heartbeat accelerates, and your nervous system goes into high alert. When the stimulating situation passes, your parasympathetic system takes over and applies the "brakes." You calm down. Your adrenaline level goes back to normal. The accelerating heart can be measured—the heart rate speeds up. When the heart rate "brakes," the heart rate slows down.

Scientists have found that the seesaw between the accelerator and the brakes or between the speed up/slow down aspect of your heart rate happens on a moment-to-moment basis. Your body, when relaxed and at ease, balances these two opposing forces. You are neither asleep (and under the dominant influence of the brakes) or overly alert and hyper-vigilant (under the dominant influence of the accelerator.) No, in an ideal state, the accelerator and the brakes balance out. If, when relaxed like this, you were to measure your heart rate, you would see that it is not changing from fast to slow to fast again very much. It is in a steady balanced state that the researchers call "cardiac coherence."

So, cardiac coherence is a state of physiological balance in which your heart rate variability is low. Obviously, from what I have just described, it is easy to guess that this balanced state of mind is good for you. You think more clearly in this balanced state. You solve problems better and your resistance to illnesses of all kinds is lower. This is a state of "low stress." You might be interested to find out another fascinating fact about cardiac coherence. You can create it yourself by concentrating on feeling positive emotions in your heart! Yes, feelings, especially gratitude and related positive emotions like love and appreciation, can and do flip the cardiac system and the nervous system into a state of balanced cooperation that is the ideal human condition.

I am reminded of a quotation from 'Abdu'l-Bahá, who says that when a thought of war comes we should combat it with a stronger thought of peace. A thought of hatred should be opposed by a stronger thought of love, and so on.[19] Now, this quote takes on a new meaning for me. When a "thought of war" comes, my heart goes into an accelerated state. I leave the state of cardiac coherence. To return to it, I must entertain "a stronger thought of love" and return my body to its ideal condition.

Besides its central role in regulating our nervous system and our emotions, Chilton Pearce argues that the heart is a bridge or link between the material plane and the spiritual. He points out that the new life of a human embryo mysteriously begins with the beating of cells that will become the heart. The new being organizes itself during gestation around the beating heart. This beating heart reflects both the unique beat of this new life and also the universal beat of all life energy to which it is connected within creation. Pearce's book delves deeply into the themes of "unity in diversity" as he reflects on the uniqueness of each person (and therefore each individual human heart) and at the same time reflects on our sameness.

With this new information in mind, the quote that urges me to cleanse my heart so that I may tap into a "wellspring of divine treasures" makes a lot more sense. My own heart—that is where I should turn for guidance, knowledge, and spiritual understanding. I am aware that the Seven Valleys text warns against blindly following other people's ideas or influence. I shouldn't worry about what other people think, whether it is positive or negative. The text tells me not to be guided with trying to fit in with my friends and certainly warns against focusing my energies on people in a negative fash-ion—having or creating enemies. No, the good news, which is also the bad news, is that I am responsible for my own spiritual development. I have no one to blame if I fail to progress and no excuses either. I have a wellspring of divine treasure in my own heart, for goodness sake! What more could I ever want? I just never thought about that phrase enough. A wellspring of divine treasure.

That would be a good question to ask people on a televi-sion quiz show: Where is the wellspring of divine treasure? Can you imagine the answers people would give? Califor-nia? Las Vegas? The Riviera? In the Bermuda Triangle? Nope. In you, in me, in our hearts.

Questions: The Heart, a Wellspring of Divine Treasure

1. Notice any negative emotions or internalized anger or resentment you may be feeling. How can you rid yourself of these destructive emotions?
2. Who do you need to forgive?
3. Notice that sometimes we see in others the faults that we ourselves carry buried out of awareness within our own hearts. What faults in others bother you the most? Do you have these faults?
4. Are you afraid to follow you own heart because of disapproval from others? Do you feel the need to please others rather than be true to your own heart?
5. Do you tend to rely most on reason or heart wisdom? Can you balance them and synchronize them in ways that optimize your effectiveness in the world?

Meditation 3: Heart Coherence

As in previous exercises, place yourself in a time and place to meditate. Assume a relaxed posture, close your eyes, focus your attention on your breath, imagine yourself breathing "through" the center of your body, around the area of your heart, notice the feeling in inhaling and exhaling. As you focus on your heart area, create an emotional feeling of gratitude by "just feeling it" or by recollecting some time or place or something for which you feel grateful. Breathe "into" this grateful feeling in your heart. Continue for some time, bringing your attention passively back to the feeling of gratitude if attention wanders. Continue for a time.

Journal Entry 10: Seek at Every Moment

In their search, they have stoutly girded up the loins of service, and seek at every moment to journey from the plane of heedlessness into the realm of being.[20]

At every moment, seek to journey into the realm of being. Be at every moment aware, spiritually aware, spiritually awake, spiritually mindful; not unaware, asleep, or heedless.

At every moment, try, Pat, to keep your attention focused on this moment. Now, and now, and now. There is a whole movement afloat in holistic and alternative medicine that is based on training people in the spiritual practice called "mindfulness." Scientific studies have shown many positive benefits of this practice. Practitioners have lower stress levels, higher resistance to illness both mental and physical, increased immune system function, faster recovery from illnesses and injuries, and so on.

I am noticing that the quotation I am meditating about tells me to seek at every moment the "realm of being," not the realm of *doing*. I remember that I began my journey vacuuming with thoughts racing around inside my head while I argued with myself—heedless.

To become mindful now, I can focus my attention inwardly and attempt to stay present, to be in my body, to allow myself to just be here, now. To be mindful is to just be me and not identify myself with my thoughts. I am not my veils. I am not the heedlessness wrapped around my own luminous soul. I am the luminous soul. This is true for everyone!

To live in the moment is surprisingly difficult. I am always spinning fiction in my head with my noisy, feeble reason. To refocus inwardly away from thoughts, I can concentrate on my breathing and I can shut off sensory awareness for a few minutes. I can go inside myself and center and just focus on my breath going in and out. Sometimes, I say a small prayer as I do this—a prayer with each breath. This is a technique based on Herbert Benson's work.

Today, as I meditate upon this quote, I am also reminded of how much I have been influenced by the work of John Kabat-Zinn. In his book *Full Catastrophe Living: Using the Wisdom of Your Body and Mind to Face Stress, Pain, and Illness* he writes,

> . . . *behavior and feeling states can be driven by the play of the mind's likes and dislikes, by our addictions and aversion. When you look, is it not accurate to say that your mind is constantly seeking satisfaction, making plans to ensure that things will go your way, trying to get what you want or think you need at the same time trying to ward off the things you fear, the things you don't want to happen? As a consequence of this common play of our minds, don't we all tend to fill up our days with things that*

just have to be done and then run around desperately trying to do them all, while in the process not really enjoying much of the doing because we are too pressed for time, too rushed, too busy, too anxious? . . . We live immersed in a world of constant doing. [21]

I am aware of how many of my clients say they don't want to focus their attention inwardly because they will hear admonitions to do more things, good things really, but still do things: "You should go on a diet, you are too fat," or "You should quit smoking," or "You are drinking too much," or "You need to get yourself together."

While it is true that it might be a good idea to do these things that help your body, don't stop the spiritual practice just because you hear this inner voice criticizing your habits. Your body will come around once you have come to a greater understanding of your own mind and spirit. You are not your body and you are not your problems. You are not your addictions. You are not your bad habits. You are not your mistakes, shortcomings, or failures. No matter how many problems you have and no matter what you may have done in the past, you are still pure spirit and light at your core. Not knowing that may be driving you to all the things that you think are not right about you! Please don't turn away from the inward journey. Please don't think you have to be "worthy" to go on this journey. No one is worthy and everyone is worthy because at the core we are all light and love. Remember, it is just what is wrapped around your soul that is the problem. Unwrapping the veils can take time. Don't worry. Stay focused. Just try. Then see what happens after that.

Questions: Seek at Every Moment

1. Sometimes I think of the journey inward to the "heavenly homeland" as a pathway with many possible detours. I see a path through the woods with all sorts of offshoots and switchback pathways. Sometimes I have wandered way off my own spiritual pathway, thinking that this situation or this problem was "an exception to the rule." It is OK to lie, or fake it, or not pray, or do what I feel like doing, or do what is easy, convenient, expedient, will look good to others, and so forth. I am afraid this list could go on and on. Have you ever wandered off your inner pathway? Did you know you were doing that? Why did you do it? How do you get back on the pathway?

2. I also think of the spiritual pathway as being shaped like a big spiral seashell. I spiral up the shell toward higher and more subtle levels of understanding, but always enfolded within this upward movement is the wisdom of the past, the wisdom deep within, and the ultimate goal of finding my heart's hidden treasure. The "hidden" treasure is not lost or buried. It is me. I am the shell, the movement, the treasure. My awareness moves me around and around this shell, sometimes

nearer to my heart's wisdom, sometimes farther away. Can you identify with this movement? Recall times that you felt closer to your heart's hidden treasures. What spirals you away from these treasures?

Summing Up the Valley of Search

It seems as if I have made some progress. I began with a belief that spiritual progress was important and possible. I formed an intention to try to progress spiritually. Nevertheless, I found myself unable to focus my attention inwardly and found I had fears of what I might find "in there." Because of that, I often relied on my reasoning powers and ignored the wisdom coming from my heart. This led to a multiplication of fear-based veils that separated me from my spiritual core. My prayer life had become so marginal to my daily life as to be nearly nonexistent.

Despite beginning so far out of touch with spiritual resources—my major source of moment-to-moment strength and resilience—I made a commitment to at least try to place my spiritual journey first and to take the action needed to pursue it with fervor, ardor, and determination. I read and understood that patience with myself is needed. I understood that I need compassion for all, and I am one of the all.

By the end of the first valley's meditations, I was getting really excited about the idea that my heart is a wellspring of divine treasure and the idea that aid from the invisible realm is always at my side.

The whole process went from feeling overwhelming and out of my reach to being a strong feeling of happiness and energy within my heart. I feel something very good inside of me waking up. It actually feels like an awakening is taking place. I am not making that up.

In the next chapter, I'll move on to the next valley, the Valley of Love. The steed of this valley is pain, a subject all too familiar to me and to many of us on planet Earth in the twenty-first century.

Stage Two: The Valley of Love

. . . When the fire of love is ablaze,
it burneth to ashes the harvest of reason.
—BAHÁ'U'LLÁH, *THE SEVEN VALLEYS*

In the Valley of Love I continue my spiritual quest that began in the first valley, the Valley of Search. In that valley I learned to turn my attention and awareness inward and slow down the pace of my life enough to have time to devote to inner awareness. I learned that material reality can become a teacher to my heart if I remain spiritually awake during the parts of my day that demand attention to practical affairs and everyday chores. I learned to set my intention to progress spiritually at the beginning of each day. As I have done this with more and more ardor—that is, enthusiasm and dedication—I have experienced an inner awakening that is bringing me new insights into my own emotional life, my relationships, and my identity as a spiritual being. A synergy is growing between my belief in my heart's wisdom and my actions of relying on this wisdom. Keeping my attention focused on the task remains a challenge. However, as my attention is more focused inwardly at all times and my intention to take responsibility for my own inner life becomes more clear and firm, I find myself engaged in a kind of spiritual "rewiring."

I learn that whenever negative emotions arise, I can focus inwardly to correct them rather than focusing the feelings outwardly and blaming others. In this valley I learn that when I am "triggered" I am living in the past. I learn that when I am anxious, I am living in the future. In this valley I learn how to live in the present. I learn more of the details of how to shift out of negative emotional states that lower my state of consciousness and take me out of the present moment, away from spiritual joy and happiness. I notice some clear and easily definable shifts in my perception from judgment to compassion. As I do that, I find myself tapping into a huge and surprisingly intense wellspring of joy and happiness.

In the past, before this journey began, I would often feel an emptiness inside. Sometimes I thought I was hungry or lonely, or yearning for something or someone. Maybe I would find someone or something in the material world that for a time would fill this emptiness. I might say at that time I "loved" this thing or even this person who for a time seemed to fill this empty void. But this kind of love is a passing thing. This is not the lasting, abiding, spiritual joy of which this valley speaks.

In the Valley of Love, when I am really spiritually tuned in, I feel this same empty place inside me overflowing with spiritual joy! Of course, it doesn't last for long. Naturally, it doesn't last. It could, but it doesn't because, well, you'll see. The ego, at least my ego, doesn't give up easily. Because it doesn't, the steed of the Valley of Love is pain. Even as I turn to God with devotion, I can still be ensnared by the "eagle of love." I must learn in this valley to make myself "as naught," as nothing, so that I can then enter the next valley, the Valley of Knowledge, where my inner eyes are opened.[1]

Journal Entry 11: Spiritual Joy

I have just come from a conference near Harrisburg, Pennsylvania, where, for the first time, I read aloud from the Seven Valleys and from my journal. Tonight I feel so happy inside, so happy I can actually identify with this passage from the Seven Valleys. It begins at the very end of the Valley of Search and transitions to the Valley of Love.

> *And if, by the help of God, he findeth on the journey a trace of the traceless Friend, and inhaleth the fragrance of the long-lost Joseph from the heavenly messenger, he shall straightway step into the Valley of Love and be dissolved in the fire of love. In this city the heaven of ecstasy is upraised and the world-illuming sun of yearning shineth, and the fire of love is ablaze; and when the fire of love is ablaze, it burneth to ashes the harvest of reason.*[2]

I taught an audience of over one hundred people to meditate. The silence filled the large, formal lecture hall with a stillness like music. Among all those hearts searching inside for the light, I truly began to experience a sense of spiritual ecstasy.

After five minutes, I started to ask them to "awaken," but no one was ready. After another five minutes the audience returned from the inner world to the outer world, and we all talked about the change in the atmosphere. Everyone was more relaxed. I could hear the change in my own voice as the speaker. I was calmer and more confident because I had become centered in my own spirit. Some in the audience spoke of feeling refreshed. Some had asked questions of their heart and had received confirmations. Others spoke of the fear of turning inward. One man said he had a history of emotional traumas, and he said he has always tried to avoid turning inward. He had become afraid of himself, he said, afraid of his own emotions.

I reminded him of the fact that these negative emotional states are veils between him and his own heart. He is his heart and its love and light. He is not the veil, not the fear, not the old feelings of shame, or anger, or resentment. These are just feelings. It is possible to notice them arising and let them pass through. Stay with the process. You are pure spirit, pure love, you have nothing to fear.

During the last few minutes of the meditation, I could feel the love in the room getting stronger. It was so wonderful to be part of a large group of people all praying silent prayers, all looking inward to find their true selves.

Speaking to others about these things has brought me an inner joy that surprises me. I had been very nervous about sharing these innermost thoughts and struggles with others, but even the vacuuming entry from my journal was laughingly and lovingly received.

I guess I could feel the presence of God in that room. For the two hours I spoke, I felt the hearts of the listeners in the room and my own heart were attuned. My body was tired after the presentation, but deep inside, my spirit was and still is jumping for joy. I can't explain it. I don't even want to try. I am comforted by the text that says, "when the fire of love is ablaze, it burneth to ashes the harvest of reason."[3]

I am reminded of the journal entry on ardor—how I am supposed to search with intense heat, excitement, fervor. Now, tonight, I actually feel this excitement. I am so happy and grateful to be doing this work. Just sharing a few journal passages seemed to help some folks feel OK to be stuck or distracted or busy, busy, busy, too. They seemed to come away from the talk with a renewed determination to pray and meditate. The bookseller said there was a "run" on *The Seven Valleys and The Four Valleys.* This is my hope—that more and more people will turn to this inspiration that, for me, is so powerful.

Since I decided to make this journal a book, I have been wondering what I would say when I decided to move past the Valley of Search. I honestly have never before felt this intense spiritual joy that I feel tonight. I know a lot about the pain this valley talks about. The text says "the steed of this Valley is pain," but until tonight, intense spiritual joy has not registered so clearly. Tonight I am the traveler who the text says is "unaware of himself, and of aught besides himself."[4]

Earlier today, I reminded the audience that 'Abdu'l-Bahá would always ask people, "Are you happy?" I have to say tonight, I am so, so happy.

I can feel the pull to analyze it. Maybe it is because . . .

"No, Pat," I tell myself. "Just be aware of the happiness. Notice it. Be grateful for it. Just be, Pat. Just Be." The quiet seems like bliss.

Tonight before bed, as my husband and I sat silently on our side porch in the still darkness, now back in a meditative state, he quietly whispered, "It doesn't get any better than this."

I smiled a small, soft smile and answered, "No, it doesn't." I went to bed later in this floating state of joy, hoping to keep floating all night long.

Questions: Spiritual Joy

1. Think of one of your happiest times. Hold that feeling of happiness in your heart. What do you notice?
2. Try to stay in this happy, peaceful state of mind all day. What happens in your relationships when you greet others this way?
3. How does your reasoning, thinking mind react to strong feelings of joy and happiness? Does it try to stop them, limit them, analyze, or otherwise interfere?
4. Is it OK to be happy?
5. Can you—do you—give yourself permission to feel deep gratitude for life?

6. Have you told those you live with, work with, and associate with that you are grateful for them? Do you show appreciation to others? How does it make you feel when you acknowledge others?

Journal Entry 12: Abounding in Sanity

To merit the madness of love, man must abound in sanity.[5]

Merriam-Webster's Collegiate Dictionary says that to abound means "to be present in large numbers or in great quantity." It also means "to be filled." Synonyms include "teem" and "overflow." So, once again I am reminded to try to overflow with sanity. That is the main message of today's meditation. I am learning now to hold these lessons in my mind as the day progresses and to try and apply their wisdom to daily happenings. It is amazing what is revealed to me as I apply this process.

Today my husband and I went to our boat on the Chesapeake Bay. It is springtime, and all sorts of things need to be done to get ready for sailing. "Spring commissioning" it is called—to give all the scrubbing, scraping, painting, and arranging a dignity deserving of the sport. We have been at it since early morning. I am taking a break now under a shady tree near the dock. It is late afternoon, and I feel spiritual gravity setting in. I am tired, and my husband just spoke to me in an irritated tone because he was anxious about an electrical problem on the boat.

The boat is small, only twenty-six feet long, not large for a cruiser. Still, her size belies her complexity with air conditioning and heat, indoor plumbing, microwave, TV set, and radio. Then there's the diesel engine that always needs maintenance. In the past, I have expressed some pride that I taught my husband to sail. Now, since my ego is undergoing these size-reduction treatments, I realize that my husband does all the chores on the boat while I sunbathe and suggest "improvements" that mainly fall to him. "Let's paint the bottom, let's change the oil, let's install new mattresses." "Let's," after all, really means "Why don't you?" He never points out this fact. He just works along and claims to enjoy it, and meanwhile our little getaway vessel comes to life.

So today this small irritation in his voice over the fouled electrical system should be instantly forgiven. Instantly, come on, Pat. But it isn't. No, I am more aware of my inner life now, and I feel anger rise within me like a bird of prey ready to strike. Beady-eyed and hyper-focused on my prey, it took but one moment of the wrong inflection in this sweaty man's tired voice for me to spread my talons and lower my head, ready to strike. Inside my head, I could hear myself ready to respond, "Well, you don't have to *yell* at me." I might have snapped, but I didn't do that today. I almost did, though. Instead, I retreated to this quiet bench to think and write.

I was guided here by this tiny but now more easily trusted voice inside me saying, "Uh, Pat, I think I notice anger rising within you. I really think I do. Whose problem is this?" I don't like that question because now I know the answer is always "Mine." So, before I made a fool of myself, I told my husband I needed a "break," and I headed for this bench. Nice, I need a break from all the work *he* is doing.

Before this inner journey and journaling began, I would have been absolutely *sure* the problem was *his. He* talked to *me* in an angry voice. Now I say to myself, "Did he? Are you absolutely sure he did? Or was he hot and frustrated that his wiring was fouled up? Did his tone really have anything to do with you?" I have to fess up to myself as I look back on it from this bench.

No, he was annoyed that after all his work, the wiring was still fouled up. He might have been somewhat annoyed with me because he kept asking me to leave so he could concentrate, and instead of leaving I kept making "helpful" suggestions. Things like, "Do we really need the electricity?" Or, "Maybe you need to take a nap." Sometimes I am such a wife, the kind of wife men complain about in bars over a beer. A nap? How is that going to fix the wiring? Am I going to fix it while he naps? Not on your life!

Anyway, at least I didn't start a fight. I am sitting on this bench wondering why I reacted, or nearly reacted, with anger. I question my perceptions, and as I sit puzzling, he comes to my bench and explains in a now relieved tone of voice that all the circuits on the port side of the boat are working but the entire starboard side has blown a fuse. "Worked last week," he says. "I'm going to go and get another fuse box." He is calm, clear what the problem is—the fuse box.

This process is really getting eerie now. I look at him wide-eyed, like an owl, barely moving. Blow a fuse is what I was about to do. "Yes, dear," I say, grateful I dodged my inner demon. "I'll be right here. Take your time."

"Triggers," I called them in *It's Not Your Fault*—old patterns, old habits of emotion that distort reality. Today I could feel myself being triggered by the frustration in his voice about the wiring problem. I felt myself react. "A man is yelling at me," my innards told me, and I was ready to strike.

I remember an explanation of this whole phenomenon was so clearly and powerfully depicted in the independent film *What the Bleep Do We Know?* Scientists, physicians, mental health professionals, and mystics combined their talents to try to get the world to tune in to the hidden inner workings of the mind/body and perception. In the movie, a woman with Post-Traumatic Stress Disorder is triggered at a wedding of a friend. She has been hurt by her ex-husband, and her emotional scars play themselves out for the viewer as she reexperiences her own traumatic wedding memories superimposed upon the current reality of the wedding she is attending. She is "triggered," and the moviemakers do an amazing job of depicting with cartoon-like illustrations the inner workings of her mind/body. Chemicals called peptides that are associated with negative emotions zoom all over her body like evil demons. They alter her perceptions, send her into a distressed state of mind, and bring her into a defensive posture. The movie explains that people can get addicted to these peptides associated with negativity. You can actually get addicted to anger, or worry, or depressive emotions. These emotions will so color present reality that you will act in ways that are literally "insane." You will project these inner feelings onto outer reality and feel that others are *making you* angry, worried, or depressed.

At least today I was a little more aware of this triggering process. I intervened before I let my old scars contaminate our lovely afternoon. After the explanation of the electrical problem, I quickly apologized to my husband for leaving so abruptly. He said he had not noticed. He was just wondering whether or not we needed a new fuse box. Wow, a new fuse box. If only people with emotional scars could just get a new fuse box! Maybe that is a good way for me to look at this spiritual quest. At least in part, I am trying to rewire. I am trying to interrupt old, negative, destructive, and definitely unloving ways of being and install new wiring.

Today I am aware that the "red alert," the fire alarm for the faulty wiring, was a strong negative emotion. In the past, I used to think that there were times and occasions in which such blasts of anger were justified. After all, I would reason, *you* did this or that so *therefore* I have a right to scream at you.

Nope. Not anymore, I don't. I have a right to address the problem, to discuss, to refuse to be hurt, or exploited, or harmed. But just allowing myself to get triggered because of the past and then blasting someone in the present—nope, that is not OK. That is emotional irresponsibility, emotional pollution, toxic waste dumping. I realize I have a long way to go.

Questions: Abounding in Sanity

1. Have you ever felt as if you needed a new emotional fuse box? How often do you "blow a fuse"? What are your triggers? Be as clear and detailed as you can about situations that trigger you. Make a list of your triggers.

2. Have you ever found yourself full of anxiety, worrying about things that might happen? Do you spin what I call negative future fiction? Before public talks, I always spin positive future fiction. I imagine the audience deeply engaged in the message and interacting with me with interest. I find when I picture negative fiction, the audience looking bored and judgmental, I panic. I can't think straight. For the most part, my public talks go well. Can you think of examples in which your positive mental practice affects your actual performance in a good way? Can you think of the opposite—times you imagine failure and either do fail or simply give up before you try?

3. Do you ever categorize and judge people based on just one or two external characteristics (such as smoking a cigar or dressing a certain way)? Think of the things you use to categorize and judge like money, neighborhood, education, and so forth. Can you imagine life without this kind of judgment?

Journal Entry 13: Emotional Triggers

I had lunch with Kim the other day. Kim is the heroine in *It's Not Your Fault* who tells about her healing journey in some detail. We got into a discussion of heroic life and spiritual practice. It crossed my mind that readers who had read Kim's story in the first book would be curious about her life now. I thought it would be instructive to see that the healing journey is part and parcel of one's spiritual journey.

Since the publication of *It's Not Your Fault,* Kim has gone on to become a financial advisor with a large Fortune 500 company. She is living with her daughter and is practicing lots of healthy lifestyle changes such as good nutrition, exercise, and spiritual practices such as prayer and meditation. She has become a leader in her self-help group—an "elder," she says to me with a smile. While at first she found the role surprising and intimidating, she is now aware that she has much to teach others. Her own journey has taught her many lessons.

Kim wrote a letter to me to respond to some questions I asked her as I was thinking about this book. I asked about her experiences in sharing her story after the publication of *It's Not Your Fault* and about her new job and how it has affected her. I also asked her to comment on her own healing journey now, especially focusing on triggers.

She said that her progress in the world of work has increased her self-esteem and has given her a sense of pride in her accomplishments. She feels much more in control of her own life and is able to notice when triggers affect her emotionally. That is the good news. The bad news is that she still struggles with triggers on many fronts nearly every day. She is coping well, but it is an ongoing challenge. She mentioned that any social situation that is threatening to her may lead to an internal experience of fear. She finds it difficult to be assertive because she has to overcome the moment of fear that precedes her assertive stance. She says that once she experiences fear, it can lead to an internal triggering of a flood of bad memories—memories of other fearful events in her past. There are other social triggers, too. Being the focus of too much attention, being criticized in a punitive way, being treated unjustly are just a few of the social situations that can still trigger Kim. She also mentioned that negative emotions just seem to "spring up" spontaneously sometimes. These experiences used to frighten her, leading to internal triggering of that "domino effect" of more fear-producing memories. One fear leads to another fear—an emotional biology that is the legacy of her childhood abuse experiences.

However, when I see Kim now, I can hardly believe that these internal experiences she speaks about really occur. I believe her, of course, but her outward appearance and her behavior do not betray her internal struggles. She is good at containing her inner storms and presenting a youthful, upbeat, always-ready-with-a-joke appearance to others. It makes me think about how important it is to treat other people, even strangers, with kindness and compassion. We never know what may be going on inside them. For Kim, encountering a sales person having a grouchy day or an anonymous driver with road rage can snap her into that split second of fear that may open the floodgates of internal distress. The sales clerk won't know. The angry driver won't know. It makes me wonder how many times I have caused others distress without ever knowing it.

Questions: Emotional Triggers

1. Do you practice kindness and compassion in all of your social situations? Are there times when you think it isn't necessary to be kind and compassionate?

2. Have you ever triggered someone emotionally so that their emotional reaction was so strong it didn't seem to fit the social situation? Look back on the incident now. What may have been going on inside the other person? What was going on inside you?

3. Triggers can be both internal and external. Fear is both a trigger and a response to a trigger. Write or talk to others about your own fears.

4. Do you feel safe in all the places in your life—at home, at work, with others? If not, what needs to change to create a feeling of safety? Is it an "inside you" change, or do others need to be less aggressive, less judging, less blaming, and so forth?

Journal Entry 14: Spiritual Courage

A lover feareth nothing and no harm can come nigh him:
Thou seest him chill in the fire and dry in the sea.

A lover is he who is chill in hell fire;
A knower is he who is dry in the sea.

Love accepteth no existence and wisheth no life: He seeth life
in death, and in shame seeketh glory.[6]

I have been looking back over Kim's letter to me. I find her so amazing. She answers my questions straight from her heart. I admire her more and more every day. She is a walking, talking bundle of spiritual courage.

It is morning on the bay. I am floating on our little boat. The motion is so calming. I see the sun sparkling on the water. I see the tree-lined shoreline, and I spot a few birds leisurely gazing down at the water, scanning for breakfast. Inside my heart, I am calm today, feeling good that I am learning things. It is so hard to overcome old inner habits. I am trying to be more aware of my own triggers on a moment to moment basis. I really got such a clear idea of how often this emotional flooding can happen after I saw the "*Bleep* movie," as we refer to it around our house. When my husband finds himself triggered, he refers to the animation of the nervous system in the wedding scene of the movie. The animation makes nerves look like big green elephant trunks. The trunks associate into patterns that become our nervous system networks. To change our habits of mind, thought, and behavior, these networks have to rearrange themselves. In the movie, the "trunks" move to undo the old nervous system networks and form the new ones. "It's my trunks," he says when it happens. "I am just still trying to move those big green trunks."

I am, too. And to make matters worse, I can add to the faulty wiring—the trunk problem—the fear that everyone in the world is going to see these defects inside of me when they read this book that I am writing. I feel these thoughts blowing across the calm of my inner self like a freshening breeze on the bay. The quiet breeze is gaining momentum. I hear feeble reason loud as a trumpet.

"What are people going to *think* of you?"

"How will they judge you?"

"Think of how clear it will be to everyone that the depth of your spiritual understanding is so shallow."

"Everyone will see your faults. The *whole world* will see them!"

Feeble reason is so amusing—and grandiose, too. It is a delusion to think that the whole world is interested in my shortcomings or, for that matter, inclined to buy this book.

In response to feeble reason's clamor, I reread the passage I have chosen to meditate on today:

A lover feareth nothing and no harm can come nigh him:
Thou seest him chill in the fire and dry in the sea.

A lover is he who is chill in hell fire;
A knower is he who is dry in the sea.

Love accepteth no existence and wisheth no life: He seeth life
in death, and in shame seeketh glory. To merit the madness of
love, man must abound in sanity.[7]

I guess a lot of people might think I am crazy to be exposing my inner world by writing about it this way. I read on:

To merit the bonds of the Friend, he must be full of spirit.
Blessed the neck that is caught in His noose, happy the head that
falleth on the dust in the pathway of His love. Wherefore, O
friend, give up thy self that thou mayest find the Peerless One,
pass by this mortal earth that thou mayest seek a home in the
nest of heaven. Be as naught, if thou wouldst kindle the fire of
being and be fit for the pathway of love.[8]

So, that's it, then. I don't care what people think. . . . Well, at least I am trying not to care. The deepest part of me feels very happy doing this and talking about these things. The more I share my inner limitations and the wisdom of the Seven Valleys, the happier I feel inside. No, not in a worldly sense, what I'm saying and doing here doesn't make sense. But isn't that the point of this valley? The Bible tells us to lose our life so that we may find it. "Spiritual courage," I will call it—a force that overcomes fear.

Questions: Spiritual Courage

1. Courage is needed to overcome fear. In previous questions you were asked to make a list of fearful situations and things. Now go back to your list of fears and, with a courageous outlook, think again about how to overcome these fears. Do it first using "feeble reason," trying to think rationally of ways to overcome your fears.
2. Now spend some time meditating more deeply. Pick just one of the fear-producing people or situations, and while you are meditating ask about how to overcome this fear. What do you notice about these two ways of trying to overcome fear?

Journal Entry 15: The Steed of This Valley Is Pain

> *Now is the traveler unaware of himself, and of aught besides himself. He seeth neither ignorance nor knowledge, neither doubt nor certitude; he knoweth not the morn of guidance from the night of error. He fleeth both from unbelief and faith, and deadly poison is a balm to him. Wherefore 'Aṭṭár saith:*

> *For the infidel, error—for the faithful, faith;*
> *For 'Aṭṭár's heart, an atom of Thy pain.*

> *The steed of this Valley is pain; and if there be no pain this journey will never end. In this station the lover hath no thought save the Beloved, and seeketh no refuge save the Friend.*[9]

I have been talking for a while now about triggers and fear, and I have been trying to create safety in my life in every moment. This is so often a painful process. The passage I just quoted tells me that pain, especially emotional pain, is part of my spiritual journey. The passage reminds me of an old television show called *Mission Impossible*. At the beginning of each episode the hero would receive a tape recording that described a mission. A man's voice would come on the tape. His deep, authoritative baritone would spell out the consequences of doom and destruction that would result if the task at hand were left undone. Nevertheless, the hero was never forced into action. At the end of each recording, just before the tape self-destructed, the mission commander would say, "Your mission, should you choose to accept it, is to . . ." It was always something that sounded impossible, and it was always up to the hero to decide whether to accept the mission. It occurs to me that the point is not what the mission was, but the "should you choose to accept it" part.

In this Valley of Love, my "mission impossible," should I choose to accept it, is to stay in a state of mind in which I continually and unremittingly emanate love from the inside out. My task is to do this even though I have emotional scars, pain, triggers, fears and all the rest.

I am back at the dock of the marina again today, sitting on the same bench where I realized I needed rewiring, and I am remembering my presentation at the conference in Harrisburg. After my presentation in which I demonstrated the meditation exercises, some people approached me and complained that they had difficulty focusing. They said that they kept hearing inner chatter about the future or that their mind would wander into the past.

I know that people who suffer from anxiety live in the future, in the land of "what if?" I stumbled in there in the last journal entry when I wondered what people were going to think of me when they read about all of my shortcomings. In my imagination, I could see an inner vision of people's faces scowling as they read my words. I could see their faces screwing up in disgust, scowling, shaking their heads and mumbling, "This is garbage. What a bunch of horse manure! I can't believe people publish this stuff and, worse yet, people buy it and read it!" Oh, I could go on and on like this. This tirade of disdain flows so easily from the pen.

No matter how often I tell my anxious clients that their thoughts can't prevent the problems they fear or change the future they imagine, they just don't believe me. They go right on worrying and planning and plotting a future that never materializes. It is like the joke about the guy on the street corner who is clapping his hands and whistling day and night. Another man walks up to him and asks him what he is doing. "Keeping the elephants away," he answers. "There are no elephants around here," the other man replies. "I know," says the elephant chaser. "That's because I keep clapping and whistling!" Those who are anxious *believe* their future-oriented negative fiction, and upending it can definitely seem like mission impossible.

Then there is the seemingly all-powerful dragon of the past, which, as we have already seen, casts the spell of negative fiction on the most beautiful moments of present reality. It is just as hard not to believe it. Sitting here peacefully at the dock, writing about triggers from the past and watching the ripples on the water, I am suddenly distracted by two men who are approaching me. They are walking fast and talking loudly. Each holds a large cigar, and they puff between noisy guffaws of laughter. They both hold a green-sleeved drink can that I assume to be a beer. As they pass by me, one loudly proclaims, "Whaddaya think, Joe? Do ya think this bench has our name on it?" They plop themselves down on a bench beside me, puffing their cigars, blowing smoke, taking possession of the space. I overhear one of them say, "Those new racers are so light and so fast. They make them out of carbon fiber, and those Kevlar sails, well, hell, it's not even a race, ya know." Now a third man approaches, and the town crier of the duet calls out, "Hey, Tom, grab ya Colt 45 and slap on an end cap and you got it. You're done. There's room for three on this bench." As they sit and puff, the decibel level increases and I find myself squirming and thinking of moving. My mental chatter has begun. It isn't pretty. I am not pleased to have my meditation interrupted. I say to myself, "Humph, this bench has MY name on it, dudes, and I am being LUMINOUS! (Expletive deleted.)"

After some stewing about in this direction, I don't actually slap myself in the face, but I mentally grab hold of myself. I now refocus. Gee, I am getting really tired of that word. I realize—duh—that everything in material reality is here to teach me something. So, what about now?

I am aware that loud men are a trigger for me most of the time. Today the universe adds the cigar and beer, just in case I might miss this line into my past. I feel anger rise. "Who do they think they *are*?" I say to myself. "I have half a mind to go over there and give them a piece of my mind." My thoughts continue in this vein.

And then I note the phrase, "peace of mind . . . Come back, Pat. You are off again into the land of unreality. How quickly it happens, how easily. Come back."

I feel put down by these men, dismissed, put upon. I must ask myself: are they really doing that? Is it true? Am I sure? "No," I answer, "they are having fun." They are "living large," as they define it. They are happy. Of course they feel they own the bench. Why not?

So now, inside myself, I feel a shift. Aren't I being little miss party pooper? Aren't I the church lady here, mentally snubbing my nose at these guys with my holier-than-thou attitude? I don't even *know* them. What right do I have to think badly of them?

Now I see their families appear, a gaggle of children being herded along with balloons and colorful sand buckets and shovels. The wives are grinning from ear to ear. They look so excited to be there, and I hear them say to the men, "Is it ready? Is it gassed up?" They are getting ready to go for a boat ride.

Now I begin to see a different picture. The scumbags with the beer bellies have now morphed into devoted family chums out on holiday, finally able to afford a boat. They and their families look as if they are proud to be at this marina. Maybe they have had to work a long time to afford the boat. Now I see the men are actually kind of cute—endearing, even. It would be easy to walk up to them, talk sailboats, Kevlar, fiberglass.

So once again, the same lesson comes back to me over and over. My attention is key. Staying present is key. If my emotions turn negative inside, I need to *look inside* first. "Inside first, inside first"—maybe I could do a needlepoint and hang it on my refrigerator.

I still have to go through the Valley of Knowledge before I get to the Valley of Unity, where it will be clear to me that "all the variations which the wayfarer in the stages of his journey beholdeth in the realms of being, proceed from his own vision."[10] This is my never-ending mission impossible, to keep this wisdom always clearly before me.

Questions: *The Steed of This Valley Is Pain*

1. Triggers are unique to individuals. Not everyone is triggered by the same events, circumstances, and situations. What are your triggers? Do you know? How about the triggers of your most intimate friends—do you know how to help them when these sensitive areas are activated?

2. A wise woman once said to me, "Don't judge your own insides by other people's outsides." What does this mean to you? Do you ever compare yourself with others as you perceive them and decide that you are better or worse than they are? Can you see how this process interferes with knowing yourself and knowing others from the heart?

2. This story of my own ability in this situation to shift from judgment to love is referred to as a "teaching story" by a remarkable school near Washington, DC, called Tai Sophia Institute. The school runs a program called "Transformative Practices." I learned so much from them by attending just one of their introductory sessions at which "teaching stories" were shared. Write a teaching story about how you were able to overcome a trigger situation of your own. What was the key that allowed you to shift into love and compassion for yourself and others? Can you share this story with others with love and humility?

3. What is it like for you to share a teaching story?

Meditation 4 – Healing Meditation

This is a very old meditation that has healing properties.

Prepare for meditation as in previous exercises. Notice your body, posture, and breath. Focus on your breathing now and as you do so, pay attention to your pain or trouble. As you do so, answer the following questions about your pain or trouble and try to visualize these aspects, adding each in turn. Each will be in the form of:

If your trouble or pain had a_____what_____would it be?

For example, If your pain had a size, what size would it be? Picture your pain that size now. If your pain had a shape, what shape would it be? Picture that size and shape now. If your pain had a color, what color would it be? Picture that size and shape and color now. Continue in this manner adding any descriptors you can think of. Definitely include texture, temperature, smell, sound, and weight. Once you have your trouble visualized in this way, allow it to "sit" in your body for a moment while you shift your attention to another question.

What is your favorite color? Imagine a bright light of this color shining above your head. Now imagine this colored light emanating a laser beam aimed directly at your pain shape. See that light permeating in and around and through your pain shape. Now see the light as growing brighter and stronger and filling your whole body. See it shine in and around and through you, every cell, every speck of you. Continue in this manner and notice what happens to your pain shape.

A True Story – A Teaching Story

The summer before my fortieth birthday I noticed that I was having difficulty running or even walking fast on a treadmill. I felt old, very old. I remember thinking, "I think this is what it feels like to be eighty."

Try as I might to "get in shape," exercise only made me feel worse—more tired, more drained. I began to worry that the "heart thing," my leaky aortic valve, which had been bad from birth, was causing problems.

I went to see my cardiologist and told him of my change in energy. He sent me for an exercise echocardiogram, and the results were alarming. My ejection fraction, or the amount of blood my heart was pumping, was significantly lower than expected. It might, he thought, be nearing the time when the valve needed to be replaced. That would mean open-heart surgery, but we wouldn't know for sure without doing a cardiac catheterization. I was scheduled to have one done within a few weeks.

In the meantime, I did the things one might imagine: I made a will, put together a scrapbook for my kids, visited friends and family. I remember spiritually "ramping up," as I called it. I knew that if I had to have an operation, I would need to work with the process and not allow my fear and panic to rule. I decided to make it a spiritual challenge.

I don't remember exactly how it came about, but early in the process I focused my mind on one of the Hidden Words of Bahá'u'lláh:

> *O Son of Man!*
> *For everything there is a sign. The sign of love is fortitude under My decree and patience under My trials.*[11]

I practiced memorizing this verse, saying it over and over again. The day of the cardiac catheterization seemed to come all too soon. I mentally clung to my little prayer like a life preserver in a stormy ocean. I hoped, of course, that we would find surgery would not be necessary.

"Patience under My trials."

Once the test was completed, the doctor came to me while I was still lying on the hospital table and said, "Don't worry. It isn't an emergency situation." I breathed a sigh of relief.

Then he continued, "It can wait until tomorrow!"

"Fortitude under My decree."

I went back to my room and called my family to tell them the news. The Hidden Word I had memorized was now running through my mind nonstop. Believe it or not, I felt peaceful, confident, and actually happy! I felt that I was in a no-lose situation. If I died, well, it was the will of God, and I had had time to prepare. And, of course, if the surgery was successful and my heart valve got fixed, I would have a whole new lease on life.

The sign of love.

That evening, my husband and children came to visit. My oldest son told me jokes to make me laugh, and my youngest brought a piece of soap he had carved into the shape of a heart. He said, "When you wake up you can wash with this and remember how much we love you."

Later in the evening, my mother, brother, and sister came to see me. My brother was solemn and dressed in a black suit. He held a bouquet of flowers. When I saw his funereal attire I said, "Wow, you really are a get-ready-ahead-of-time guy!" and I started laughing. Suddenly aware of what he had done, he laughed too.

That night, after my family left, the nurse came into the room at about eleven o'clock with my medicine. I said, "What is that?"

She said, "Something to help you relax."

I said, "I am relaxed."

She said, "No, you're not, you're having open-heart surgery in the morning."

"I know," I said. "But I don't need a sleeping pill."

She said, "It's Valium." I guess she thought that would be enticing.

"No thanks," I said. "I'll just say my prayers and go to sleep."

She looked at me with a mixture of disdain and skepticism.

"Are you refusing the medication?" she asked.

I nodded my head affirmatively. "It will interfere with my concentration," I said calmly.

She shook her head in disgust and said in a stern and reprimanding voice, "I will be back in an hour, and if you're not asleep you will take it." And she clomped her nurse shoes out the door.

"Patience under My trials . . ."

The next thing I knew it was six o'clock in the morning, and I was being prepared for the surgery. I kept repeating my prayer.

I was later told that the surgery had gone smoothly, without a hitch. I woke up on the ventilator with the same prayer still running through my mind. I adjusted quickly to the obvious fact that I was not in heaven. Machines were humming and wires were running everywhere. I looked like a carburetor. I closed my eyes and said my prayer over and over and visualized myself sailing on the Chesapeake Bay. I could feel the beat of my heart calming and—yes—still beating!

"For everything there is a sign."

I was out of the cardiac care unit in record time and back in my room, where, for about three days I experienced the most amazing spiritual experiences of my life. I felt as if I could travel outside my body and go into a universe that was beautiful and expansive and full of light. The more I moved out into this beauty, the more joy and elation I felt and also paradoxically, a deep peace and calm.

I was taken aback by these experiences. What was this? Had I nearly died or something? I asked my surgeon if there had been any times when it seemed as if I would not live. He said no, the operation had gone unusually smoothly, there had been no problems. I couldn't figure it out. I recovered so quickly that I was out of the hospital in less than a week. I returned to work in about ten weeks. The doctors had found no need whatsoever to give me any blood transfusion. I still remember this experience as one of the happiest times of my life, but until now, I have never told anyone about it. I thought people would think I was crazy!

The whole experience has led me to think deeply about the true meaning of physical life and death and about spiritual life and death. The Bible says in Luke 9:24, "For whosoever will save his life shall lose it: but whosoever will lose his life for My sake, the same shall save it."

I am grateful that I have had the opportunity to experience this spiritual mystery so deeply, dramatically, and intensely. And now, in times of stress both large and small, I hear my inner voice chant, as if on automatic, "The sign of love is fortitude under My decree and patience under My trials." I wonder what my night nurse would think of that!

Love is the secret.

&

This story reminds me of my favorite passage from 'Abdu'l-Bahá's writings. He speaks of the love that holds the universe together. If you read the following passage aloud slowly, it will "blow your mind" as we used to say in the 1970s:

> Know thou of a certainty that Love is the secret of God's holy Dispensation, the manifestation of the All-Merciful, the fountain of spiritual outpourings. Love is heaven's kindly light, the Holy Spirit's eternal breath that vivifieth the human soul. Love is the cause of God's revelation unto man, the vital bond inherent, in accordance with the divine creation, in the realities of things. Love is the one means that ensureth true felicity both in this world and the next. Love is the light that guideth in dark-

ness, the living link that uniteth God with man, that assureth the progress of every illumined soul. Love is the most great law that ruleth this mighty and heavenly cycle, the unique power that bindeth together the divers elements of this material world, the supreme magnetic force that directeth the movements of the spheres in the celestial realms. Love revealeth with unfailing and limitless power the mysteries latent in the universe. Love is the spirit of life unto the adorned body of mankind, the establisher of true civilization in this mortal world, and the shedder of imperishable glory upon every high-aiming race and nation. . . .

O ye beloved of the Lord! Strive to become the manifestations of the love of God, the lamps of divine guidance shining amongst the kindreds of the earth with the light of love and concord.[12]

Concluding Thoughts

I have seen in my own experience that the steed of the Valley of Love is pain, and I accept this pain as a necessary part of my spiritual growth and development. I know that pain, fear, old negative learning, future fears, and anxieties all are part of the human condition, but all can interfere with my ability to abide mindfully and confidently within a conscious state of peaceful, happy, loving, spiritual awareness. However, I see that all of my life is really a "teaching story." Doing this work, writing this book, helps me to see that all of the tests and difficulties I have encountered in life have prepared me to do this work. I see that my own spiritual journey doesn't end. This work is a beginning for me and, I hope, for others who read it.

Next I will move on to the Valley of Knowledge, where one of my favorite teaching stories appears. I have read it over and over to myself in times of pain. It is the story of "seeing the end in the beginning." I will present it in its entirety twice, first as part of one of my journal entries, where I will include questions for meditation and then in its original context in the appendix.

I hope you are reading slowly and meditating on the passages from the Seven Valleys. These inspired words can unlock the mysteries "long hidden in human hearts."[13] I hope you are either journaling, or talking with others about your insights, or both. Remember, you are in the process of spiritually "rewiring" your brain, and that takes time and practice, practice, practice.

Stage Three:
The Valley of Knowledge

Repeat the gaze: Seest thou a single flaw?
—BAHÁ'U'LLÁH, *THE SEVEN VALLEYS*

In the previous valley, the Valley of Love, I learned many things. The biggest thing I learned was not to immediately trust my own perceptions of others when the perception is negative. I learned that many things about me can interfere with my ability to love others and myself with constant, unremitting compassion. Things such as old scars or old learning, anxieties about the future, and triggers can all alter my perception of present reality in ways that distort it radically away from truth and into a misperception based on my own issues. I learned that triggers can be especially potent because they can arise suddenly, outside of my own awareness, and can form a veil that will take my attention away from the wisdom of my own heart.

In the last valley, I learned that "teaching stories," as I called them, can help me anchor my new spiritual understanding and can help me remember the spiritual lessons I am learning. I also experienced the joy of sharing teaching stories with others. At the conference where I shared the truth of my human weaknesses and limitations and my quest for inner truth, the audience responded with compassionate understanding. They could identify with my struggle. I, in turn, experienced a flood of joy and ecstasy that I had never known before. This experience made me so excited about this book and its potential. I see now that a process is emerging in which personal truth-telling within a group of spiritually likeminded individuals can help all of us grow. I believe that we can all depend upon the guidance of the sacred scriptures of the world's religions, and we can share these wisdoms with each other openly in a spirit of mutual compassion and understanding with the intention of helping each other and ourselves to grow spiritually. This from-the-inside to-the-outside and back-to-the-inside spiritual dynamic is a potent force for personal transformation.

The process began with my turning inward with the *intention* to live from my spirit and my heart each moment of every day. Then I turned my *attention* to sacred writings—in this case, the Seven Valleys—and meditated upon them. I have found that if I do this in the morning, I can behold the awareness of my meditation in my mind as the day progresses. This *action* of "tuning in" to inner awareness as the outer material events of the day unfold allows me to find within each moment a spiritual lesson. Even the most mundane affairs, even the simplest tasks, can be a tutor to my soul if my *belief* is strong and my intention is clear and focused. Then all of my actions may become infused with spiritual potency. Then the hidden mysteries in my heart begin to unlock. Then my own hidden potential begins to emerge.

Life gets exciting when I feel buoyed along the river of the spirit. I begin to feel an overflowing wellspring of support surrounding me. The entire process is a continuous surprise, however, as my stunned and shrunken ego stands in the shadow, awestruck by life emerging *without* its tiresome interference. When I live more from my heart than from my head, when I rely on spiritual strength instead of my ego, when I realize that a limitless reservoir of spiritual strength is available to me at all times, I live life much differently than when I think I must rely only on myself, my ego, my reasoning mind alone.

My ego used to rattle in my head like a radio sportscaster at a horse race.

"Now they are coming around the first mile post, Pat's lagging behind. Seems she needs a bit more flogging to catch up. Run faster, Pat! Race harder! Compete, compare! You are *failing!* You are *winning*! But soon you will be failing again!" The ego runs a race that never ends in anything but exhaustion, defeat, or despair. It feeds on fear, and I run to escape the fear.

Spiritual life, I am learning at a level deeper than I have ever known before, is a life of calm comfort and safety at the deepest levels of my being, regardless of what may be going on in my outer life. It is a life of spiritual joy and confidence regardless of life's circumstances. I feel within me an inner peace I have never known so intensely before. I have such an assured sense that life is as it should be. Just this understanding is a tremendous gift. I feel a huge relief that I can't explain. Negative emotions like worry, guilt, and so on, are presently at bay.

Now I will move on to the Valley of Knowledge, which Bahá'u'lláh calls "the last plane of limitation" before the Valley of Unity.[1] In the Valley of Unity, I am told, my inner eyes will open and I will experience an even deeper level of spiritual transformation. Before I get there, though, I must pass through this valley, the Valley of Knowledge, where I will remind myself once again to see that everything, even what appears to be a trial or tribulation or a test, is a spiritual blessing.

It has been hard for me to write about this valley because I have spent many years in the past wandering around in it. All three of the valleys I have just discussed are valleys within the planes of limitation, or grades of self. The patience needed in the Valley of Search and the pain of the Valley of Love all intermingle for me within the Valley of Knowledge, where I need to constantly be aware of seeing the "end in the beginning" and where I need to learn to remain steadfastly on the "straight path" at all times. Needless to say, my aim has not always been straight. Therefore, I have doubled back again and again to pain and patience, lessons to be learned again and again.

Still, though, the concept of spiritual blessings being embedded in everything, especially in those experiences that seem like failure, is an idea that is embodied within me and my children in such an indelible and unquestioning way that our family conversations would seem illogical, perhaps even "out of touch" to one without this type of outlook. Both of my sons, now grown men, are in the movie industry. They are self-employed, the oldest as a producer, the younger as an art director. The pace of their lives is fast and unpredictable. Deals are on, deals are off. Movies are being funded—oh, no, they are not. The schedule is this, no it's that, and so on. Within the past few months, my older son informed me that I should get ready to go to a big, prestigious film festival in Europe. Boy, did I get ready! New clothes, French books galore, even a ball gown with a train! I was going to be ready for this!

Then my son called, and I answered the phone, "Bonjour!"

"Ah, you're killin' me with that French, Ma. We are not going to Europe," he said.

"Oh, I thought it was a for-sure thing," I said.

"Well," he said, and I am not making this up, "I thought it was too, but as it turns out, it isn't happening, and I know it is a *huge* blessing."

I answered, "Well, I am sure it is!" And while I knew it was, there was that ball gown. He had moved on though and I got on board the blessing train.

My children have taught me many spiritual lessons. Years ago, when it was time to go to college my son applied to an Ivy League school. It was the one and only school he applied to. When the rejection letter came, he walked into the kitchen with it and told me to hang it on the refrigerator.

"Well, honey," I said, certainly surprised, "OK, but don't most people hang their *acceptance* letters on the fridge?"

"Mom," he said, "treasure your failures. Treasure them. Because embedded within every failure is your next move toward success."

Astounded, I hung the letter on the fridge. Subsequently, I was given many opportunities to answer questions from curious friends and relatives who saw the "I am sorry to inform you" letter hanging there in all of its splendor. No shame. No, nothing to hide. See the end in the beginning.

As for me, I have already mentioned an "end in the beginning" story in the introduction to this book. I explained that I had written a whole manuscript, sent it in to my editor, realized it was terrible, and I quit, and it was all a great blessing—all of this process is part and parcel of this valley.

So, here in the Valley of Knowledge, Bahá'u'lláh will tell you the story that sustains me and sustains my family through good times and bad. In the Valley of Knowledge, Bahá'u'lláh tells us his own teaching story. I have read this story so many times I can recite most of it from memory. I have even told it many times to my clients in my own words when I have counseled them in times of emotional pain and suffering.

Bahá'u'lláh tells us of a man who is in so much emotional pain that he decides to end his life. The man goes out one night to commit suicide and is chased by "watchmen," or the police of the times. They chase him right into a brick wall! He hits the wall and, "forgetting his life," the story says, he scales it and then throws himself over it! He drops smack into the garden of happiness, love, and delight!

Bahá'u'lláh then explains this teaching story. He tells us that when we leave this Valley of Knowledge we will realize that our lives are perfect for us just as they are. The text says,

> *The wayfarer in this Valley seeth in the fashionings of the True One nothing save clear providence, and at every moment saith: "No defect canst thou see in the creation of the God of Mercy: Repeat the gaze: Seest thou a single flaw?"* [2]

Before this most recent "ramped up" and more focused phase of my own spiritual journey, I could not understand the passage, "Seest thou a single flaw?" My goodness, I could have made a shopping list three miles long of all the flaws I could see in myself, in others, and in the world.

That was then. Now when I hear myself criticizing something or being negative, I become aware of the passage from the next valley, the Valley of Unity, which explains that "all the variations" I experience in my journey "proceed from [my] own vision." [3]

I have structured this chapter a little differently than the ones before it or after it. Since Bahá'u'lláh is telling a story, I have not added a great deal of my own story to it. Instead, I am just going to present the story slowly, in small segments, with some explanation to make the story clear to modern ears. So, in this chapter, my journal entries are mostly just brief summaries or comments on the text. My life and yours are our own teaching stories. As you read this valley's story, think about how you can apply its wisdom to your own life.

Each section of the story will include questions or meditations to help you do this. It might be best to read the whole story through once as it's presented in context in the appendix. Then, as your heart guides you, move through the story at a slower pace, perhaps taking time to pray and meditate on the wisdom locked within it as it reverberates to your own life.

Keep in mind that like all good teaching stories, the story itself has many layers of meaning. Certainly it is just a plain good story with a hero, a quest, and a victory at the end. It is a story of redemption, too, of the need for the human ego to give up before spiritual guidance can prevail. The story teaches us about our lives on earth, but it also teaches us something about our relationship with our Creator. The lover who longs for his beloved can also be seen as us, longing for reunion with our own spirit and with God. So, I will begin.

Journal Entry 16: Bahá'u'lláh's Teaching Story Begins

There once was a lover who had sighed for long years in separation from his beloved, and wasted in the fire of remoteness.[4]

This passage reminds me of all the people in my life that I have loved and who, for whatever reason, have been separated from me. Some just didn't love me back. Some loved me, but they were separated from me by distance, illness, even death. And this passage reminds me of my own longing for spiritual peace. It reminds me that my heart has been searching for so long, and even though my own spiritual pathway, the Bahá'í Faith, has brought me untold comfort and guidance, I am aware that still I have doubted. I have not paid attention. I have erred and gone astray. I have failed to practice virtue or have become fascinated with things, people, career, money—you name it. All these things have separated me from my true beloved who awaits within me.

The story continues:

From the rule of love, his heart was empty of patience, and his body weary of his spirit; he reckoned life without her as a mockery, and time consumed him away. How many a day he found no rest in longing for her; how many a night the pain of her kept him from sleep; his body was worn to a sigh, his heart's wound had turned him to a cry of sorrow.[5]

Questions: Bahá'u'lláh's Teaching Story Begins

1. Have you ever felt like a hero?
2. Have you ever been in emotional pain? Have you ever felt sad, depressed, anxious, and miserable?
3. The passage speaks of the heart's wounds. Do you have a wounded heart? Are these wounds wearing you out, causing you pain, sapping your joy?
4. Do you know others with wounded hearts? How do they wear their scars? Do they present themselves as angry, defensive, negative, complaining?

5. How do you wear your scars? How does a hero wear scars?

Journal Entry 17: Hitting Bottom

The text of the story continues,

He had given a thousand lives for one taste of the cup of her presence, but it availed him not. The doctors knew no cure for him, and companions avoided his company; yea, physicians have no medicine for one sick of love, unless the favor of the beloved one deliver him.[6]

Notice that no one seems to understand this man, and no one seems able to help him. The situation seems hopeless. In this state of mind, this man is so miserable to be around that people avoid his company. Basically, this poor man finds no help for himself either from the best doctors of his day, nor from friends, family, or anything else. This man is suffering, plain and simple, and he is stuck in this suffering and can't see a way out. He gets so worn down with all of this that he decides to commit suicide, which the story delicately describes this way:

At last, the tree of his longing yielded the fruit of despair, and the fire of his hope fell to ashes. Then one night he could live no more, and he went out of his house and made for the market-place.[7]

So, this man has "hit bottom." He has given up all hope of ever getting what he wants, and so he decides to take matters into his own hands in the most radical way possible. He sets out for the marketplace in the middle of the night. We readers presume that he is going to jump off a bridge or something, but before he can get very far with his desperate plan, the night watchman comes and starts chasing after him. He is out past curfew, and the police are out to stop him. First one watchman starts after him, then others join in. The story continues:

> *On a sudden, a watchman followed after him. He broke into a run, with the watchman following; then other watchmen came together, and barred every passage to the weary one. And the wretched one cried from his heart, and ran here and there, and moaned to himself: "Surely this watchman is 'Iszrá'íl, my angel of death, following so fast upon me; or he is a tyrant of men, seeking to harm me." His feet carried him on, the one bleeding with the arrow of love, and his heart lamented. Then he came to a garden wall, and with untold pain he scaled it, for it proved very high; and forgetting his life, he threw himself down to the garden.*[8]

The Bible says that to find our life we must first lose our life. In other words, to find our true spiritual identity, we must give up our worldly ideas of who we are. In some self-help traditions in this country this idea is expressed as "hitting bottom." 'Abdu'l-Bahá refers to the "insistent self" that we must overcome to find spiritual light.[9] All of this advice is similar in its basic notion that our self-centered egos are not to be trusted as a guide in our lives. Only when we give up the insistent self do we find true and lasting peace and happiness. Many of us—I for one, and the hero of our story for another—have had to suffer many hardships in life to finally find the wisdom to "give up."

Questions: Hitting Bottom

1. What needs to change in your life in order to open the doors to your heart?
2. What do you need to give up in life?
3. What is your garden wall, in other words, who or what do you keep slamming into? What is an example of a spiritual lesson you are trying to learn. Can you see this lesson being presented to you in many different ways in your life?

Journal Entry 18: Seeing the Light

And there he beheld his beloved with a lamp in her hand, searching for a ring she had lost.[10]

It has always struck me as significant that not only was our hero, who was "bleeding with the arrow of love," driven to his heart's desire by adversity, but also that the love of his life was suffering adversity when her greatest blessing plummeted willy-nilly, literally out of the sky into her lap! Had she not been out in her garden in the middle of the night "searching for a ring she had lost," his spectacular entrance back into her life would have gone completely unnoticed by both of them! I always picture her, driven awake by anxiety about this silly lost ring. Can you imagine her thoughts that night? "How could I be so stupid as to lose a ring right off my own hand? I know I had it at lunch time, but where in the world could it have gone? I can't believe I am up at this hour. Surely it could wait till morning, but . . ."

How usual a thing could it be for this maiden to have lit up a lantern after everyone else was sleeping and to go trooping outdoors alone into her garden? Here we find her, hair askew, wispy robes tied haphazardly around her, down on her knees in the dirt, peering under bushes, searching under benches, finally all the way back to the garden wall. Imagine her feeling when, BAM, here comes her star-crossed love! Literally, out of the blue—no, out of the black! Yes, out of the black and blue, if you catch my drift!

Questions: Seeing the Light

1. Imagine the scene of the hero and heroine in the story. Imagine how the evening began for both of them with despair, frustration, hopelessness, confusion, despera-

tion, fear, panic, and all the rest. Then imagine how they felt when their eyes met! Imagine that moment of recognition!

2. Can you identify with this story? Which characters do you identify with and why?

3. Have there been moments in your life when you have hit bottom?

4. Do you think you still need to hit bottom in some areas?

5. Can you recall a time in your life when despair gave way to joy and when you were able to see the "end in the beginning"?

Journal Entry 19: The Wisdom of Tests and Difficulties

When the heart-surrendered lover looked on his ravishing love, he drew a great breath and raised up his hands in prayer, crying: "O God! Give Thou glory to the watchman, and riches and long life. For the watchman was Gabriel, guiding this poor one; or he was Isráfíl, bringing life to this wretched one!" [11]

Thus Bahá'u'lláh's teaching story ends. Now he gives us his interpretation just in case we have missed the point. This is a very key idea, because he doesn't usually go into so much detail in explaining things. Here is what he says:

Indeed, his words were true, for he had found many a secret justice in this seeming tyranny of the watchman, and seen how many a mercy lay hid behind the veil. Out of wrath, the guard had led him who was athirst in love's desert to the sea of his loved one, and lit up the dark night of absence with the light of reunion. He had driven one who was afar, into the garden of nearness, had guided an ailing soul to the heart's physician.

Now if the lover could have looked ahead, he would have blessed the watchman at the start, and prayed on his behalf, and he would have seen that tyranny as justice; but since the end was veiled to him, he moaned and made his plaint in the beginning. Yet those who journey in the garden land of knowledge, because they see the end in the beginning, see peace in war and friendliness in anger.[12]

The Bahá'í writings speak of two kinds of tests: those that are sent as blessings to tutor our souls and those that arise because we have made wrong choices. The suffering from the wrong choices often doesn't end until we make right choices, until we mend our ways. The suffering that is meant to tutor our souls is in the hands of God, and as Bahá'u'lláh's teaching story promises us, we can be sure that this suffering is really a "blessing in disguise." True saints are known to have prayed for tests. Spiritual wimps like me pray to be spared from tests!

Questions: The Wisdom of Tests and Difficulties

1. Think about your own life. Can you identify with the idea of wrong or bad choices that have led you into adversity?
2. Can you identify with tests that are blessings?
3. Are you currently in the midst of serious tests and difficulties?
4. "Mental tests" as they are called in the Bahá'í writings are often very difficult. What is a "mental test"? Have you experienced mental tests?

Meditation 5: A Favorite Prayer

I want to share my favorite prayer. I first heard it read by my own child when I had been a member of the Bahá'í Faith for only a short time. My son, a blond and freckled very young new reader, read the prayer in his high-pitched child's voice with such earnestness. It particularly struck me because he was just about the happiest, most joyful being I could imagine at the time. Hearing him pray to no longer be "sorrowful and grieved" or "full of anxiety" or to "no longer let trouble harass" him hit me as so ironic. Yet of course I thought of his future days, and I too prayed that that happy little boy would continue to be as "happy and joyful" as he was that day.

Do your breathing exercises and relax for a time. Then read this prayer and let it "sink in." Let it refresh and gladden you!

O God! Refresh and gladden my spirit. Purify my heart. Illumine my powers. I lay all my affairs in Thy hand. Thou art my Guide and my Refuge. I will no longer be sorrowful and grieved; I will be a happy and joyful being. O God! I will no longer be full of anxiety, nor will I let trouble harass me. I will not dwell on the unpleasant things of life.

O God! Thou art more friend to me than I am to myself. I dedicate myself to Thee, O Lord.[13]

Journal Entry 20: The Straight Path

"Guide Thou us on the straight path," which is: "Show us the right way, that is, honor us with the love of Thine Essence, that we may be freed from turning toward ourselves and toward all else save Thee, and may become wholly Thine, and know only Thee, and see only Thee, and think of none save Thee."

. . . "Verily, we are from God and to Him shall we return."[14]

I believe Bahá'u'lláh is saying in this passage that once I understand the need to turn away from myself and turn only toward God, I have acquired the lesson of this Valley of Knowledge. I need to stay on what he calls the "straight path" and keep focused all the time on that in order to progress. Then, he says, as I do that, I will pass through this "last plane of limitation" and come into the next wonderful, joyful valley, the Valley of Unity, where my inner spiritual perception takes over and I hear with "the ear of God" and see "with the eye of God."[15]

Questions: The Straight Path

1. What does it mean to you to stay on "The Straight Path"?
2. Are you on it? Is there anything in your life that you need to change?
3. Think of your character. Which virtues are you strongest in? Which need work?
4. How can you practice being on the straight path daily?

Summing Up the Valley of Knowledge

I don't really believe the Valley of Knowledge can be summed up. It is an ongoing process for me. I realize in this valley that there is no ending point, no black-and-white, no point at which I will be finished and done with it. There is no room for a "now I am there and I can rest" attitude within spiritual development. It is an ongoing process. The journey does not end. I am always on a learning curve, and all the valleys with all of their wisdom are always pertinent.

I try to ask for God's forgiveness each day for the times I veer off the straight path and especially if I fail to keep things between myself and my fellowman on a plane of unity and accord. I am trying, just trying, which is where I began this journey. My heart tells me that I never really know, nor will I ever know, which valley I am *in* because these valleys are not places, they are processes. I am always in all the valleys to one degree or another. I am always starting over at the Valley of Search with my prayer life resembling a parsley sprig on a turkey dinner, and I am always trying to see the "end in the beginning," and I am always trying to stay on the "straight path." I am always a human material being trying to find my spiritual core. I am always in a process of becoming, of unlocking my heart and finding its potential. And so, I am going to continue this process and share my journal as we move into the Valley of Unity.

Bahá'u'lláh's explanation of the Valley of Unity is quite lengthy compared to the other valleys he discusses. The Bahá'í Faith's main message for humankind is unity, and so it is not surprising that this valley receives lots of attention. I will be commenting on the main ideas as they stand out for me in the process of my journaling.

Stage Four: The Valley of Unity

". . . All songs are from the King."
—BAHÁ'U'LLÁH, *THE SEVEN VALLEYS*

The Valley of Unity includes the advice,

Wherefore, it hath been said for the guidance of the ignorant:

Cleanse the rheum from out thine head
And breathe the breath of God instead.[1]

For those of you who think this whole discussion is getting a little too lofty or esoteric, let me define the word "rheum" that we are being instructed to clean out of our heads. Rheum, in the simplest terms, is snot. You know, when you have a cold your head fills up with something. Another word for it is "mucus," and an even better word for it if you play Scrabble is "catarrh." That means the same thing. So far, I have talked in many different ways about the barriers we carry inside us that create a blockage between our own understanding and a full and true knowledge of our spiritual nature. I have called these barriers all sorts of lovely things—dust, veils, delusions. Now we really get down to it—snot. We are being told to clean it out.

In this valley, the text says that if you are "sick of a rheum," then "a pleasant perfume is as naught."[2] In other words, if your head is clogged, you won't be able to smell anything. So, if you are sitting right next to the most spiritual person on earth, a person reeking of divine fragrance—let's say it is comparable to the smell of a rose—if your head is all stuffy, you won't smell a thing. You won't notice. You won't perceive; therefore you won't experience it. If you don't experience it or perceive it, you will say it isn't there. As far as you're concerned, it doesn't exist! And it's all because your head is full of snot.

Notice that I am saying *your* head. I will not dwell on the fact that I have been recovering from a cold for about a month as I am writing and that I am the one who keeps saying the universe is always trying to teach me something.

So here we are in the Valley of Unity, where spiritual perception is the key. You will find that the heart is mentioned many times. It is the heart that is the home of the Master of the House. It is with the heart that we perceive His presence, because it is the heart that "contains" Him. It is heart-wisdom that will allow our sense perception to play second fiddle to our spiritual perception.

In this valley Bahá'u'lláh explains Messengers of God and their role in allowing us humans to experience the presence of God. Without these Messengers, God would be unknowable to us. The text reminds us that "No man hath ever known Him; no soul hath ever found the pathway to His Being."[3] Paradoxically, even though no one can know Him, we can know *of* Him, and we can know that essence of ourselves that is of Him. The degree to which we know Him and reflect His light determines our own level of consciousness.

In this valley Bahá'u'lláh gets very explicit about the idea that people have different levels of consciousness. Some of us have noses more clogged or less clogged than others'. He says that the way we perceive things is dependent upon our own ability to perceive and not upon creation itself. As we learned from the last valley, there is nothing wrong with creation. Repeat the gaze and you won't find a single flaw. The flaws are in our ability to perceive spiritually, and in that department—well, we all have colds to one degree or another. I know I certainly do.

If I can clear my head, that is, "cleanse the rheum" from my head, raise my level of understanding to a higher level, then I am in for a big personal transformation. In this valley I learn to look "on all things with the eye of oneness" and see the "brilliant rays of the divine sun shining from the dawning-point of Essence alike on all created things."[4]

I don't understand everything that Bahá'u'lláh talks about in this valley. And after this valley he speaks of three more valleys: the Valley of Contentment, the Valley of Wonder, and the Valley of True Poverty and Absolute Nothingness. I understand even less about those valleys. But I will present some of the ideas he talks about from all of them, because some of the ideas can be understood, at some level, by nearly everyone.

In the Valley of Unity I meditate upon the idea of the Master of the House of my heart and soul really taking over my life. I meditate upon clearing my spiritual head cold and letting my heart really be in charge.

Journal Entry 21: Light and Love Is Everywhere

> It is clear . . . that all the variations which the wayfarer in the stages of his journey beholdeth in the realms of being, proceed from his own vision. We shall give an example of this, that its meaning may become fully clear: Consider the visible sun; although it shineth with one radiance upon all things, and at the behest of the King of Manifestation bestoweth light on all creation, yet in each place it becometh manifest and sheddeth its bounty according to the potentialities of that place. For instance, in a mirror it reflecteth its own disk and shape, and this is due to the sensitivity of the mirror; in a crystal it maketh fire to appear, and in other things it showeth only the effect of its shining, but not its full disk. And yet, through that effect, by the command of the Creator, it traineth each thing according to the quality of that thing, as thou observest.[5]

I have read Bahá'u'lláh's teaching story about seeing the end in the beginning countless times. I have told the story to others many times. I have wanted to remind myself and others that what has happened or what *is* happening is all for a good reason if we can but see it.

As my life goes on, I have been learning to be grateful for many things that I used to complain about in earlier years—my heart condition, not being a ravishing beauty, the list goes on. My mind travels back to my teenage years when I was so envious of Annette Funicello, the Mouseketeer. It seems so silly now, of course, but I can still vividly recall the stab of jealousy I would feel every time her smiling face appeared on the old black-and-white television set. She always got the boy she wanted, it seemed. Not I. I had a case of insecurity that would have sunk a battleship—very painful insecurity. Then, of course, there was my envy of good schools. I used to crave ivy-covered buildings—the Ivy League. I have walked the campuses of Penn, Princeton, and Harvard, thinking "if only . . ." And then there is my bad aortic heart valve—I've had that since I was a child. Surely it was the thing that nipped my budding Olympic career in the bud. Actually, I dreamed of being the first female professional baseball player (either that or a ballerina). Oh, yes, I tell only the truth here as best I can. Had you seen me at forty years of age, you would have seen me doing both, because I was taking ballet *and* playing softball on a local recreation league team. I played first base, no less, and I was quite proud. The ballet didn't go as well. I did fairly well with memorizing the names of the body positions, but then one day the teacher said it was time to actually *do* the positions. She suggested that we begin the day's lesson by wrapping my leg around my neck. I went back to softball.

Vain imaginings, they are called. In this Valley of Unity I find that those who dwell in this land see in themselves "neither name nor fame nor rank" but find their own praise "in praising God."[6]

Tonight I am letting these words sink in, and as I do, I find myself transported to a place of amazing peace and joy inside my own heart. This is a drop of the taste of the Valley of Unity. Bahá'u'lláh calls the valleys before these "grades of self," "realms of limitation," or being, heaven forbid, "completely veiled."[7] But in the Valley of Unity, Bahá'u'lláh says, my inner perception begins to bring me awareness of the true nature of reality, which is unity, oneness. He describes it this way at the end of the Valley of Knowledge, where he says those beyond that valley do not just see the end in the beginning:

> *Nay, they see neither beginning nor end, and witness neither "first" nor "last." Nay rather, the denizens of the undying city, who dwell in the green garden land, see not even "neither first nor last"; they fly from all that is first, and repulse all that is last. For these have passed over the worlds of names, and fled beyond the worlds of attributes as swift as lightning. Thus is it said: "Absolute Unity excludeth all attributes."* [8]

The message seems so clear to me tonight. Everything is really light and love if I can just perceive it as it really is. Light and love is everywhere—it is me, you, us, creation. We are all one, but the seeming discontinuity and disunity and differences among us have to do with the receptivity of each soul and the resulting perception based on that receptivity. My own soul can reflect light and love just a little or a lot. This is my choice, and it is very dependent on my ability to believe and pay attention and work to clear the perceptual "cold" that obscures my spiritual senses. This must be such an absolutely key concept and fundamental idea to all of spiritual development because the text about this is very long and detailed and not so hard to understand either. I think Bahá'u'lláh really wants me to "get" this idea.

> *In like manner, colors become visible in every object according to the nature of that object. For instance, in a yellow globe, the rays shine yellow; in a white the rays are white; and in a red, the red rays are manifest. Then these variations are from the object, not from the shining light.*[9]

Meditation 21: Light and Love Is Everywhere

So often in this culture—that is, in the United States during the twenty-first century—we define ourselves by our attributes. We are young or old, short or tall, married or single, educated formally or not, rich or poor, Hispanic or African American or Asian. We are men, we are women, we are children. We are sick, we are well, or we are Democrat or Republican. We are in the group or out of the group, or we don't even have a group at all. In other words, all these attributes or descriptions of you and your "outer" world and groups and doings have absolutely nothing to do with the core of your being. None of it really matters. It is all illusion.

In my meditation below, I experience a moment of "oneness" as I see the reflection of the mast of the little sailboat in the water. Then a breeze comes along and disturbs my perception. Has the oneness really been altered, or is it just my perception? Meditate on the phrase "Absolute Unity excludeth all attributes."

Meditation 6: My Meditation on the Bay

The night was luminous. My little sailboat sat still and quiet in the peaceful lagoon nestled in the Chesapeake Bay. I sat transfixed, watching the reflection of the tall, white mast mirrored in the glistening silver water. It shone forth like a huge "ONE" on the breathless bay, and I thought, "Yes, one, I can feel that here, tonight. That oneness, that stillness, that peace." My heart was happy and full of love and gratitude. I silently said a prayer of thanksgiving.

As I prayed, a slight breeze began rising farther out on the bay. I watched the stillness of the water being disturbed as the wind drifted toward me. Ripples on the water's surface spread toward my place of stillness. As the waves touched my reflection of oneness, the image suddenly changed. The ripples divided the reflection into tiny bits of white, like many, many little sticks floating separately here and there, one by one. Between the tiny sticks, I could see no connection. The separateness that I saw, I knew to be false—an illusion brought by the wind. Still, my heart yearned for that oneness that had been mine only moments before. I wanted to see that, experience that, once again. To see it again, I closed my eyes.

Questions: Light and Love Is Everywhere

1. How do you feel about yourself as you reach out to more fully understand this oneness?
2. How do you feel about others as you become more conscious of humanity's oneness?

Journal Entry 22: Good and Evil

And if a place be shut away from the light, as by walls or a roof, it will be entirely bereft of the splendor of the light, nor will the sun shine thereon.

Thus it is that certain invalid souls have confined the lands of knowledge within the wall of self and passion, and clouded them with ignorance and blindness, and have been veiled from the light of the mystic sun and the mysteries of the Eternal Beloved.[10]

As I am reading and rereading about being completely shut out from the light, I am thinking about the issue of good and evil. Working as much as I do with people who have been abused as children, they almost always ask, how could God allow the abuse of a child? Why does God allow bad things to happen? Why does He not stop murder, for instance? Why does he allow lying, and stealing, and adultery, and all the rest?

As I ponder the passage above, I begin to understand more. Some people, those whom Bahá'u'lláh calls "invalid souls," are shut out from the light by passions and selfishness, and these invalids inflict harm on other people. It is interesting that He calls them "invalid" souls. When I look up the word "invalid" in *Webster's English Dictionary,* I find several meanings. They include "not well, weak and sickly; infirm." It can also mean "weak; of no force, weight, or cogency."

So perhaps extreme evil is being more completely shut out from the light of the love in the universe. The light and love is always there, always available to us, but some souls choose to close themselves off from it to such an extreme extent that they commit heinous acts.

> *In sum, the differences in objects have now been made plain. Thus when the wayfarer gazeth only upon the place of appearance—that is, when he seeth only the many-colored globes—he beholdeth yellow and red and white; hence it is that conflict hath prevailed among the creatures, and a darksome dust from limited souls hath hid the world.*[11]

Questions: *Good and Evil*

1. Meditate on what Bahá'u'lláh says about good and evil in the previous passage. Think of our world and how it would become transformed if everyone could understand what He is saying.
2. Think of all the conflicts in the world. Think of the incredible implications of this statement in terms of violence in our society, warfare, and all the other conflicts that plague us. Imagine a world in which everyone understood oneness. How would your life change if you started acting within this reality now?
3. Think about good and evil in your own heart. How can you increase the light and love in your heart?
4. How can you shift to loving others instead of judging, blaming, or criticizing?

Journal Entry 23: *Lighthearted Virtue*

O My Brother! A pure heart is as a mirror; cleanse it with the burnish of love and severance from all save God, that the true sun may shine within it and the eternal morning dawn. Then wilt thou clearly see the meaning of "Neither doth My earth nor My heaven contain Me, but the heart of My faithful servant containeth Me." And thou wilt take up thy life in thine hand, and with infinite longing cast it before the new Beloved One.[12]

My heart contains God. Wow! Now I am seeing much more clearly why it is so important to practice virtues. Virtues shine up the mirror of my soul and scrape off the dust. As I have been writing this book, all along my "feeble reason" has been nagging at me, saying, "Sooner or later you have to tell people they have to be good, follow the rules, give up all their bad habits." I have resisted doing so because until I came to this valley and thought about the idea of my heart as the home of my spirit, to me, being "good" was associated with being sort of "a drag." Not that I didn't try to do the right things, mind you. I have had enough spiritual lessons in my life to know that the straight path is ultimately the easiest, safest, and downright most pleasant path. But still, there is always that tugging in the other direction.

For instance, in the past I might have felt like having a big glass of wine to get in a "party mood." I am aware that Bahá'u'lláh discourages drinking alcohol of any sort, saying that it is so bad for you that if you really had a full knowledge of it, you wouldn't even put a drop of it near you. But, of course, I live in a culture full of bars, and to "party" is still so often to drink that sometimes I just feel like it. Before I came to embrace more fully the wisdom of this valley, I sometimes felt as if I were making a "sacrifice" when I refrain from drinking my big glass of wine. I often felt as if I were giving up something good that I wanted.

Let's consider backbiting. Bahá'u'lláh condemns it as a "grievous error," explaining that it "quencheth the light of the heart, and extinguisheth the life of the soul."[13] This amazes me. I guess it must be because it is the cause of so much disunity and conflict. But, gosh, doesn't everyone gossip just a little? It is so enticing, so appealing.

And then there is income tax. Does anyone really tell the truth when they do their taxes? I once had an accountant tell me that the laws are based on a certain amount of assumed cheating! It's the American way, isn't it?

Today this litany seems so stupid, so trivial, to me. Now I am able to say "no thanks" to drinking without giving it a second thought. I just don't want it—it makes me feel bad. And gossip, yikes, I am not going there. It makes me feel even worse. And income tax, oh please! Why tax my soul with such stupidity? Give Uncle Sam his due. I can't take it with me. But my soul, I will take that with me.

So virtue, from the point of view of making my heart a home for spiritual warmth and light, feels good. It feels comforting, safe, relaxing. It is not at all a judgmental, severe, wet blanket, fire and brimstone, church lady finger-pointing attitude. None of that stuff goes with a truly enlightened heart. An enlightened heart is light. Lighthearted! With such an attitude, laughter is always one breath away!

To be virtuous is to be lighthearted, happy. I like that.

Questions: Lighthearted Virtue

There is a wonderful book and workbook and deck of cards that teach virtues to people of all ages. It is *The Virtues Project*, by Linda Popov. Each virtue is described, and exercises are provided to help practice and focus on the virtue during the day. It is amazing to me how many virtues there are. In days gone by, the notion of studying and practicing virtues was part of education. Somehow our society and culture have gotten away from these ideas.

1. What do you think of education that leaves out virtue?
2. Whose job is it to teach you virtues, to teach children virtues?
3. Do you think "virtue" is something people strive for today?
4. How can you practice virtues in your own life?
5. Make a list of all the virtues you can think of. Rate yourself from 1 to 5 on how well you practice each one. Pick one of the virtues each day and focus your attention on putting that virtue into practice. What do you notice about your life as you do this? *The Virtues Project* will give you lots more help and hints like this to continue your virtues work.

Journal Entry 24:
Welcoming the Master of the Home of Your Heart

Whensoever the Splendor of the King of Oneness settleth upon the throne of the heart and soul, His shining becometh visible in every limb and member. At that time the mystery of the famed tradition gleameth out of the darkness: "A servant is drawn unto

Me in prayer until I answer him; and when I have answered him, I become the ear wherewith he heareth. . . ." For thus the Master of the house hath appeared within His home, and all the pillars of the dwelling are ashine with His light. And the action and effect of the light are from the Light-Giver; so it is that all move through Him and arise by His will. And this is that spring whereof the near ones drink, as it is said: "A fount whereof the near unto God shall drink. . . ." [13]

If I compare my state of mind now to what it was when I began this journey, my new state of mind is much quieter. I am accepting, noticing, being grateful, looking for the good in things, for the light. I am not arguing in my head with myself or thinking that things "should be" this way or that way. "Feeble reason" is now taking a backseat to the wisdom of my heart. My reasoning powers are certainly called upon when needed. But reason is becoming the servant of my heart-wisdom when it comes to running my life.

It is late at night as I write these words. The cares of the day do not distract me, so I hope that I can keep this attitude strong tomorrow when my day begins.

The Master of the House—I am aware of the concept of hospitality, and how I value it. I prepare carefully for guests. I clean the house, make the beds, and prepare food. When the guests arrive, I am on my best behavior, and I am conscious of their presence. I don't just do and say any old thing, but it is not planned or contrived to fool them or trick them into thinking I am someone I am not. It is just that I am happy that they are there. I am happy to be in their presence. I welcome them!

I am aware of how different I feel when I am consciously identifying myself as the home of the Creator, the Master of my heart.

I am really going to try to keep this thought in the forefront of my mind tomorrow and see how the day goes. Can I keep this awareness alive? What happens when I do? Is it difficult? Will I slip in and out of it?

Questions: Welcoming the Master of the Home of Your Heart

1. Can you try to keep your awareness of your heart as the home of your Creator alive in your mind for twenty-four hours? What happens when you do?
2. Is it difficult to keep this awareness? What takes you out of it?
3. The Bahá'í writings speak often of "remembrance of God." Perhaps this awareness of God as the Master of your heart is at least one meaning of this phrase. How do you feel when you hold onto an awareness of God? How do you feel when you forget?
4. How do your actions change when you are mindful versus when you are forgetful?

Journal Entry 25: Knowledge Is a Single Point

However, let none construe these utterances to be anthropomorphism, nor see in them the descent of the worlds of God into the grades of the creatures; . . . For God is, in His Essence, holy above ascent and descent, entrance and exit; He hath through all eternity been free of the attributes of human creatures, and ever will remain so. No man hath ever known Him; no soul hath ever found the pathway to His Being. Every mystic knower hath wandered far astray in the valley of the knowledge of Him; every saint hath lost his way in seeking to comprehend His Essence. Sanctified is He above the understanding of the wise; exalted is He above the knowledge of the knowing! The way is barred and to seek it is impiety; His proof is His signs; His being is His evidence.

Wherefore, the lovers of the face of the Beloved have said: "O Thou, the One Whose Essence alone showeth the way to His Essence, and Who is sanctified above any likeness to His creatures." How can utter nothingness gallop its steed in the field of preexistence, or a fleeting shadow reach to the everlasting sun? The Friend hath said, "But for Thee, we had not Known Thee," and the Beloved hath said, "nor attained Thy presence."

Yea, these mentionings that have been made of the grades of knowledge relate to the knowledge of the Manifestations of that Sun of Reality, which casteth Its light upon the Mirrors. And the splendor of the light is in the hearts, yet it is hidden under the veilings of sense and the conditions of this earth, even as a candle within a lantern of iron, and only when the lantern is removed doth the light of the candle shine out.

In like manner, when thou strippest the wrappings of illusion from off thine heart, the lights of oneness will be made manifest.

. . . "Knowledge is a single point, but the ignorant have multiplied it." [14]

Bahá'u'lláh explains that "the splendor of that light is in the hearts." He explains that oneness will manifest itself after all the "wrappings of illusion" have been stripped from our hearts. He explains here and in other texts that the conflicts among religions is one of the greatest barriers or veils to humankind's understanding of unity and oneness. He tells us that "Knowledge is a single point, but the ignorant have multiplied it."

The Bahá'í writings tell us that throughout the life of humankind on earth, God has never abandoned His creatures. We have always had Messengers of God who come to teach us and help us gain more and more wisdom and understanding of the divine. As history has progressed and humanity has become more sophisticated and ready for greater and deeper knowledge, successive Prophets of God have revealed more and more. So Bahá'u'lláh identifies himself as part of the succession of Manifestations of God, a succession that includes Moses, Jesus, Muḥammad, Zoroaster, and others, including some who appeared before recorded history or to peoples without written language.

The fact that humankind has never been left alone is a great comfort to me. Our hearts have always been given the knowledge needed to live within the sheltering stronghold of God.

It is painful for me to watch humanity now as it twists the true meaning of the Messengers of God and literally pits the followers of one Messenger of God against the followers of another. The Bahá'í writings explain that this is like having my right hand at war with my left or having my legs reject my shoulders. The misery of humankind at war with itself stems from a lack of knowledge of unity.

I find it physically painful and emotionally very upsetting to watch the newscasts that depict the wars that are going on now between and among various religious sects. Bahá'-u'lláh tells us that religious truth is, in essence, "a single point," and that point is unity and love. To act outside this principle is to distort the purpose and true message of the religions of God. The Bahá'í Faith is dedicated to bringing this essential message of oneness to humankind. It is dedicated to bringing peace to the world. It recognizes all humankind as citizens of one planet and as members of one human race. It does not seek to compete with or eradicate other religious pathways, but rather has as its mission the dissemination of knowledge that will increase the ability of those of all religions to appreciate their own pathway and that of others. Central to the Bahá'í way of life is the concept of the independent investigation of truth. It means that each of us is responsible to find and follow our own spiritual pathway. Each of us is responsible for ourselves, and we are not here to judge or label or categorize others.

It is clear that on the best of days, we all fall short in perfectly and completely reflecting the light of God. No one, except the Manifestations of God themselves, is a perfect being.

I have always found it meaningful to think about the fact that all the Manifestations of God were misjudged and persecuted by their fellow creatures. In fact, it was many years ago that I found myself meditating on the Pharisees in the Bible. They were a group of people who did not recognize Jesus for who he was. They tortured him and crucified him on a cross. I found myself wondering if I would have been a Pharisee. Would I have felt as if I had the answer and that this new person whom I had never heard of before couldn't possibly be a true Messenger of God?

The fact of the matter is that I actually was a Pharisee at one point in my life. In college I had been studying comparative religions. I had run across the name "Bahá'í Faith," but I couldn't find much information about it in the small library of my school. When I saw a sign hanging on a bulletin board saying that students from a neighboring college were Bahá'ís and they were going to have a meeting I called the phone number that was listed on the sign.

The young man on the other end of the telephone said that the Bahá'í Faith was the newest of the world's religions, only some 120 years old.* He told me that Bahá'u'lláh was

---

* The Bahá'í Faith was founded in 1844.

the Messenger of God and that Jesus had returned in his essence. I answered this young man with a smart aleck tone and a snippy "Well, that is ridiculous. I have a personal relationship with Jesus, and if He had come back to earth again, I would *know it.*" I slammed the phone down. I guess I thought Jesus was going to send me a personal message or something.

It was ten years later that the Bahá'í Faith again came back into my life. My best friend was a Bahá'í. I had absolutely no interest in knowing about this funny sounding faith and felt that it surely must be some kind of cult or something since it was so obscure.

My friend went on a trip to the city of Haifa, Israel. This is where the world center of the Bahá'í Faith is located, on Mount Carmel, high on the mountain overlooking the city. On the mountain is a huge gorgeous garden with amazing buildings: a sacred temple and other buildings that house the books and artifacts of the faith. The Universal House of Justice is there too, the international governing body of the Bahá'ís all around the world.

I had the strangest experience when I saw my friend's travel photos. I saw the buildings and I immediately "knew" that the Bahá'í Faith was true. My heart, that is, knew. My intellect, my reasoning side, was absolutely against it. In a moment in time, when I saw those photos, my heart leapt for joy and while it leapt, I was angry, actually angry. I stormed out of the room where the photos were being shown. I banged my hand on my kitchen counter and shouted, "I don't *want* to be a Bahá'í! I can't even say it! It sounds weird, freaky, what will people *think!*" In that moment, I think I experienced the strongest, clearest, and most memorable split between head and heart that I have known before or since.

After I calmed down, I made a plan to study the Bahá'í Faith. I must confess to secretly hoping to find something wrong with it so I could reject it. That was over twenty years ago, and when I look back over my life, I can't imagine how to express my gratitude for what I have learned. Bahá'u'lláh's revelation guides me every day. It provides a stronghold for my heart to feel safe and secure, and it provides a wealth of intellectual knowledge and good common sense that helps me understand things such as progressive revelation and the essential unity of all religions and other concepts that are so key to my life.

Is this a testimony to my love for the Bahá'í Faith? Of course it is. Am I telling you that you should be a Bahá'í? Of course not. I have no right to tell anyone what they should or should not do. That is quite literally against my religion. I do hope, though, that if your path leads you to Bahá'u'lláh, you will not be as thickheaded as I was the first time around. Many are called to the Bahá'í Faith as their spiritual development within other paths and disciplines deepens, because in so many ways the Bahá'í revelation contains explicit advice about the next spiritual steps humankind needs to tread on its way to true global peace and unity.

Questions: Knowledge Is a Single Point

1. How much do you know and understand about the many religions on the planet? Would you like to know more?
2. Do you feel separate or divided from certain groups, perhaps racial or ethnic groups, socioeconomic groups, or others? For you, what is the feeling of separateness about? Can you make friends with someone in this "other" group? If you did, do you think it would change your mind about the group?
3. Do you think unity on the planet is possible? What is it going to take to get there? How can you contribute to the process?
4. I have been talking about heart wisdom versus head wisdom. Do you think feelings of separateness from each other are products of our head, our heart, or our head and heart not working well together? Or is it from something else?

Summing Up the Valley of Unity

In the Valley of Unity the mystical and the practical meet. Unity as a concept is as profoundly ethereal as any concept can be. Everyone and everything is really one. But what does that mean on a practical level? It means a lot.

Practically speaking, unity as a functional concept is a powerful force for good no matter where you apply it. I apply it as a psychotherapist with individuals who feel unsettled within themselves, who have inner conflicts. I help them become more coherent, more unified in mind/body/spirit. I help them resolve their inner struggles, and often this involves bringing peace and unity with others, especially others in their families. Moving from the individual level to the family level, family therapy is an effort to bring unity to all members. Unity includes justice and fairness and equality of men and women with special regard for the children. Unity does not mean sameness. "Unity in diversity" is a touchstone concept of the efforts of the Bahá'ís. But the goal of unity does not stop at the individual or family level. I apply these same principles when I consult with organizations and businesses. Disunity causes dysfunction, and I try to help them achieve their maximum potential as an organization by helping them overcome the disunity. The unified, cohesive operation of the entity as a whole directly depends on the unified action of all its members.

But even that is not enough. Nations as a whole need unity and need to see themselves as part of a global unity that includes all the peoples and nations on the planet. Bahá'ís are intimately involved with the United Nations and with other groups that seek to bring this unified world vision into being.

The realization of this unified world vision is happening, of course, on many levels, both big and small. At the same time, the agonizing death throes of the old world order continue to dominate much of our news media. But underneath the sound of the guns a river of peace is slowly gaining momentum. A friend of mine is writing a book about it that he has tentatively titled "The Secret Peace." It gives me hope and determination to realize that I can be a part of this growing peace. I can do something each day to try to participate in the process of unity building that is slowly but surely unfolding.

I have taken a lot of strength and courage and a very wide, world-embracing view from the wisdom I find within the Bahá'í revelation. I have formed a strong intention to try to help others understand this wisdom, and in doing so, this book, speaking engagements, and other opportunities seem to be presenting themselves each day to help me carry out my intention. I try to keep my attention focused on my spiritual life, but I admit that this is still hard for me to do. When my mind gets tired, I am still learning to turn for refreshment to the life-giving waters of the spirit. And in terms of my actions, well, they flow as much as possible from these convictions. I have seen that as I put myself more and more into a state of mind where my head is working in concert with my heart and I am attuned to the spirit, life seems to flow, energy is available, and my heart is light and happy. I laugh a lot. In fact, I do seem to feel more and more connected to a state of mind I had as a child, when laughter came easily and I felt carefree and happy and lived very much in the moment.

In the next chapter I will attempt to enter the Valley of Contemtment. I am aware that I still have a great deal to do right here in this valley. But I do want to share some of Bahá'u'lláh's vision from the remaining valleys, some of his insights that go way beyond what I can even imagine experiencing right now.

Stage Five: The Valley of Contentment

"Only heart to heart can speak the bliss
of mystic knowers . . ."

—BAHÁ'U'LLÁH, *THE SEVEN VALLEYS*

My spiritual journey continues as I venture into the last three of the seven valleys Bahá'u'lláh describes. They are the Valley of Contentment, the Valley of Wonderment, and the Valley of True Poverty and Absolute Nothingness.

In other valleys, I have learned to identify myself as a spiritual being and I have begun to learn how to put this knowledge into practice. I have tasted what it is like to operate from my spiritual core with my head and heart in balance. I have learned that my own potential to serve the world is only beginning to unfold as I come to rely more and more on my spiritual side.

The journey up to this point has been focused on the task of identifying with spirit rather than ego as the foundation of reality in each moment of life. I have come to the realization that shifting the focus of my attention from material things to the power of love transforms everyday life. I have come to see that my attention needs to be focused always on love, and I have noticed that each moment carries within it a choice. I can always choose love—or not. My actions flow from the choices I make from moment to moment.

In this chapter I will explore what life looks and feels like when the spiritual choice, the choice to focus on love, becomes habitual. In these next three valleys, the struggle against materialism has already been won in a general sense, and some practice over time has allowed this spiritual way of living to become more ingrained. The heart is attuned to God and shines brightly, emanating the love of God to all.

What does life look like when this is going on? Bahá'u'lláh tells us that we will be filled with spiritual joy and radiance at all times, regardless of our outward circumstances. He mentions "contentment" as the best description of the fifth valley and "wonderment" as the hallmark of the sixth. In the seventh and last valley, issues such as struggling to keep the ego in check and identifying with material reality have become so irrelevant that He calls it the Valley of True Poverty and Absolute Nothingness.

Before this journey began, when I read the Seven Valleys and heard the title of that particular valley, I wondered why anyone would want to experience true poverty and absolute nothingness. It didn't sound at all appealing to me. "True Poverty"—isn't that welfare and destitution? And "Absolute Nothingness"—isn't that being dead, nonexistent? It didn't sound like anything I wanted to go through.

But as you will see, these last three valleys are character-ized by ecstasy so exquisite that it defies description. Bahá'u'lláh tells us that the beauty of these valleys is so extreme, words cannot describe it. He says, "The tongue faileth in describing these three Valleys, and speech falleth short." In these valleys outward circumstances are mean-ingless: "Although to outward view, the wayfarers . . . may dwell upon the dust, yet inwardly they are throned in the heights of mystic meaning . . . and drink of the delicate wines of the spirit."[1]

Another way to refer to these three valleys is to call them "higher states of consciousness." I have already described states of consciousness and explained that your state of con-sciousness is directly related to what you perceive to be true. Now, with the background of all that we have discussed so far, I will explain in more detail why this is true. I will intro-duce the concept of "energy" or "vibration," and we will turn to science as well as to the spiritual teachings of Bahá'-u'lláh to learn about the essence of love as a creative and healing force.

In this chapter, you will learn that you are not solid mate-rial form at all, you are not a "body." Rather, you are an en-tity that is made up of energy—energy that is always vibrat-ing, moving, in a constant state of change. "Oscillation" is the word I used to describe this on page 75.

We know from science classes in school that the whole of the universe is made up of atoms, and we know these atoms have a nucleus and that protons and electrons rotate around this nucleus in the same way that the Moon travels around the Earth. But did you know that when analyzed more closely these atoms and their parts are not really "things" at all, but rather patterns of energy? If you are curious to know more, look into the science of quantum physics. A description of its theories is beyond the scope of this book, but suffice it to say that the idea that vibrational frequencies create reality is scientifically sound. Consciousness itself is a vibration. Higher states of consciousness are characterized by higher vibrational frequencies, and lower states are characterized by lower frequencies. Emotions follow this same pattern. When you are depressed, don't you say you feel "low"? And you sometimes get so happy that you feel "high" or "pumped up."

Love has a different energy than fear or hate. The vibrations of joy are different than those of sadness or anger. So, of course, the logical question is how to transform the negative emotional states to positive ones. As you will soon find out, the answer is surprisingly simple. You combat a negative emotion by emanating its opposite. You conquer fear with courage, hate with love, and so on. In fact, positive emotions are what characterize states of contentment, wonderment, ecstasy. In this chapter you will learn that love vibrations hold the universe together, and you will see that by aligning with love, you bring healing, contentment, wonderment, and ecstasy into the world. You become a healer to the world, and you yourself are healed.

Journal Entry 26: Lights of Guidance

> *O thou dear one! Impoverish thyself, that thou mayest enter the high court of riches; and humble thy body, that thou mayest drink from the river of glory. . . .*
>
> *Thus it hath been made clear that these stages depend on the vision of the wayfarer. In every city he will behold a world, in every Valley reach a spring, in every meadow hear a song. . . .*
>
> *Peace be upon him who concludeth this exalted journey and followeth the True One by the lights of guidance.*
>
> *And the wayfarer, after traversing the high planes of this supernal journey, entereth the Valley of Contentment.*[2]

Bahá'u'lláh ends the Valley of Unity with the passage above and transitions from it into the Valley of Contentment. Notice that the wayfarer who has reached this point is already on the right path and beholding a world in every city and hearing a song in every meadow. In other words, the wayfarer who reaches this level of understanding has allowed God to guide and direct his or her life.

When I think about the phrase "lights of guidance" from the passage, I am reminded of my days as an amateur airplane pilot. I took lessons on a tiny two-seater. Next to me, my instructor sat, tensely grabbing the controls at key moments. I was quite nervous the first time I was out in the plane in the dark. I couldn't imagine how we would ever find the airport. From two thousand feet up, the earth appears black and formless. The shapes of trees and forests and rivers and buildings are indistinguishable from one another, except where lights shine up and outline a certain shape. We had been flying in southern New Jersey, in the farmland. We had been out too long, and night fell suddenly along with a thick cloud cover that settled more quickly than we anticipated, engulfing us in darkness while we were still miles from home.

Our instruments gave us a pretty good idea of where we were, but still, I can remember the feeling of joy and relief that surged through my body when I finally spied the runway lights that night. They were bright blue and ran in two parallel lines like strings of precious gems, gleaming in the darkness. We were running perpendicular to the runway, so we needed only to alter our course somewhat to get into the "the pattern" required to land. We circled the little airport and lined ourselves up with the lights. We glided slowly to the ground, tucking ourselves safely in between the strands of blue lights. The moment the wheels touched the ground and the plane nestled into the run toward the hangar, I knew I was safe at last.

Bahá'u'lláh has shown us the runway lights in His first four valleys. He says, "Peace be upon him who concludeth this exalted journey and followeth the True One by the lights of guidance."[3]

When we do that, when we trust the process, believe, follow, stay on course spiritually, we land in a new place, and "in every meadow hear a song."

The emphasis of the first four valleys has been lining up to the runway, if you will—getting ourselves in line spiritually. I have written at length about taking responsibility for my inner life, about treating others with kindness and compassion, and about learning to focus my attention on the inner life of the spirit.

Now in the next three valleys, I will learn to allow the love of God to heal my soul. I will learn to experience the inflowing of peace of mind in the Valley of Contentment. I will feel the astonishment and joy of the Valley of Wonderment. And finally, if I stay on the path, I will enter the Valley of True Poverty and Absolute Nothingness and feel a type of ecstasy that defies description.

I find myself feeling very happy writing about these valleys now, although I found it impossible a few months ago. The insight that freed me to write was the realization that the first four valleys have to do with me doing for others and the last three with accepting what God is doing for me. I guess that proves that I have trouble loving myself. How often I have chided my clients who have a low self-image with the phrase from the Bible, "Love your neighbor as yourself." I tell them that this principle can also be reversed to "Love yourself as your neighbor." So, in these last three valleys, I am learning that I am loved, and I am learning to accept that love as it comes flowing into my heart.

Questions: Lights of Guidance

1. Do you love yourself? Do you wish yourself well?
2. Are you ready to accept tremendous blessings?

3.   Is it OK with you if these blessings change your life?

Journal Entry 27: Turning Sorrow Into Bliss

Bahá'u'lláh says that in the Valley of Contentment,

> *the spiritual wayfarer feeleth the winds of divine contentment blowing from the plane of the spirit. He burneth away the veils of want, and with inward and outward eye, perceiveth within and without all things the day of: "God will compensate each one out of His abundance." From sorrow he turneth to bliss, from anguish to joy. His grief and mourning yield to delight and rapture.*
>
> *Although to outward view, the wayfarers in this Valley may dwell upon the dust, yet inwardly they are throned in the heights of mystic meaning; they eat of the endless bounties of inner significances, and drink of the delicate wines of the spirit.*
>
> *The tongue faileth in describing these three Valleys, and speech falleth short. The pen steppeth not into this region, the ink leaveth only a blot. In these planes, the nightingale of the heart hath other songs and secrets, which make the heart to stir and the soul to clamor, but this mystery of inner meaning may be whispered only from heart to heart, confided only from breast to breast.*
>
> *Only heart to heart can speak the bliss of mystic knowers;*
> *No messenger can tell it and no missive bear it.*
>
> *I am silent from weakness on many a matter, For my words could not reckon them and my speech would fall short.*[4]

This passage is striking to me. I am meditating on the idea that only the heart can speak of things in this valley. Only "from heart to heart" can these "songs and secrets" be whispered "from breast to breast." How, I am wondering, is this communication from heart to heart happening? If not through words, then how else would it happen? I have found a way to think about the energy of this valley from an unlikely source—a book about the science of water.

I have been reading Masaru Emoto's *The Hidden Messages in Water.* Dr. Emoto is a scientist who works in Japan. For many years he has been studying the scientific properties of water. His work has shown that molecules of water are affected by the thoughts, words, and feelings of human beings.

Dr. Emoto studies water molecules under a microscope and takes pictures of water crystals. He studies the effects of different conditions on the shape of the crystals of water. Believe it or not, his work shows that when water is taken from a polluted stream, the crystals that are produced are malformed, misshapen, and lack symmetry and beauty. He has found that when this same water is exposed to human beings who are purposefully sending the water emotions of gratitude and love, the water crystals change shape! The deformed crystals become beautiful, like jewels. How can this be? Dr. Emoto says,

> *Existence is vibration.*
> *The entire universe is in a state of vibration, and each thing generates its own frequency, which is unique. . . . My years of*

research into water have taught me that this is the fundamental principle of the universe.

It can be said in just three words, but for people who have never heard them, these are very difficult words to understand.

Even this table? This chair? My body? How can everything that can be seen and touched be vibration? It is indeed difficult to believe that things that you can pick up with your hands and examine—things like wood, rocks, and concrete—are all vibrating.

But now the science of quantum mechanics generally acknowledges that substance is nothing more than vibration. When we separate something into its smallest parts, we always enter a strange world where all that exists is particles and waves. . . . The entire universe is in a state of vibration, and each thing generates its own frequency, which is unique. . . .

. . . Human beings are also vibrating, and each individual vibrates at a unique frequency. Each one of us has the sensory skills necessary to feel the vibrations of others.

A person experiencing great sadness will emit a sadness frequency, and someone who is always joyful and living life fully will emit a corresponding frequency. A person who loves others will send out a frequency of love, but from a person who acts out of evil will come a dark and evil frequency.[5]

This idea that existence is vibration and that the universal energy is associated with the idea of consciousness is not unique to Dr. Emoto. Scientists from many different disciplines are grappling with how to understand consciousness as it applies to quantum physics. If you search the shelves of bookstores, you will find many books on this topic. The movie *What the Bleep Do We Know!?* examined this idea, and the group of scientists, mystics, and neuroscientists who created this independent film have a Web site that can be visited (www.whatthebleep.com). The site lists books on this topic as well as information about the group's yearly conference. One of the books they recommend is *The Quantum Brain*, by Jeffery Satinover.

Dr. Satinover describes the history of quantum mechanics and applies his understanding of it to a new way of looking at humans and their brains. He describes human beings as "quantum amplifiers."[6] His notion is related to my basic premise that choosing, believing, and paying attention to something has the potential to alter reality. The effects are possible because of the quantum nature of matter and the fact that at any given moment a sea of possible realities exists. At any given moment, one out of many realities emerges. The emergence of the reality you experience has a lot to do with the ideas we have been exploring—that is, it depends upon your beliefs, your choices, your intentions, and your attention.

The science behind all of this is very complex and difficult to understand. Richard Feynman, a genius and master of quantum physics, said, that he could explain how quantum mechanics works, but explaining it did not really make it understandable. It defies understanding based on how we see and understand the world at this present time. In fact,

Einstein himself struggled with quantum physics. Dr. Satinover quotes him as saying, "This theory reminds me of the system of delusions of an exceedingly intelligent paranoiac, concocted of incoherent elements of thought. . . . If correct, it signifies the end of physics as science." [7]

What is it that has everyone confused? It is the fact that quantum events cannot be precisely predicted. The best that science can do is predict a *probability,* or, in other words, scientists can sort of guess what may happen given a set of circumstances. The guess acknowledges that mechanical determinism, or cause-effect does not operate on the quantum level. This randomness or chance that is built into the universe certainly leaves open the idea that consciousness has the power to transform.

After more than two hundred pages of describing in lucid detail the history and physics of quantum mechanics, Dr. Satinover's book ends with a chapter titled "God, Free Will, Consciousness, Morality, Religion and Belief, The Future, Society." I will leave you to read Dr. Satinover's book for yourself, but the point is that quantum physics and its key concept of everything always being in a state of not only vibration but of "possibility" makes the bridge between spirit and science. You, as a spiritual being, as a "quantum amplifier" have the ability to change the world!

I am reminded now of an event I found to be quite curious. It happened to me many years ago. I was taking a bath. My son, who was about three at the time, walked into the bathroom, as three year olds sometimes do, and made a solemn pronouncement completely out of the blue: "Mom, you have power, you have love." I remember looking at him and wondering where in the world that sentence came from. As I stared at him in amazement, he said, "Can I have a peanut butter and jelly sandwich?" Possibilities, in every moment, there are a sea of possibilities.

Questions: Turning Sorrow into Bliss

1. Since the world is made up of infinite possibilities and since you have free will to choose among these possibilities, you have the ability to join the creator in the act of creation. This is a power that lower forms of life, such as animals and plants, do not have. Do you feel the power of your own love? Can you think of a time when you transformed a situation or a relationship by using your capacity to love? What happened? Tell the story.

2. It is not necessary to understand quantum mechanics to understand that love is both an emotion and a source of transformative power, but quantum mechanics proves that old ideas of materialism and determinism are wrong. The world is not just all set up like a machine that is going to run with or without you. You make a difference, a big difference every moment of every day. Your beliefs, intentions, choices, and attention affect reality in fundamental ways. Think about your own beliefs. Do you realize that nothing can be true if you don't

believe it to be true? Do you realize that anything is possible if you believe? Apply these ideas to your own life.

Journal Entry 28: Awareness

O friend, till thou enter the garden of such mysteries, thou shalt never set lip to the undying wine of this Valley. And shouldst thou taste of it, thou wilt shield thine eyes from all things else, and drink of the wine of contentment; and thou wilt loose thyself from all things else, and bind thyself to him, and throw thy life down in His path, and cast thy soul away. However, there is no other in this region that thou need forget: "There was God and there was naught beside Him." For on this plane the traveler witnesseth the beauty of the Friend in everything. Even in fire, he seeth the face of the Beloved. He beholdeth in illusion the secret of reality, and readeth from the attributes the riddle of the Essence. For he hath burnt away the veils with his sighing, and unwrapped the shroudings with a single glance; with piercing sight he gazeth on the new creation; with lucid heart he graspeth subtle verities. This is sufficiently attested by: "And we have made thy sight sharp in this day." [8]

I am aware now that this passage is telling me that seeing a new creation, being in a constant state of awe, appreciation, and gratitude for creation, is all a matter of being able to be aware and perceive correctly with my heart. Bahá'u'lláh calls it a "lucid heart." Lucid has three meanings: (1) rational, mentally clear, (2) clear and easily understood, and (3) emitting light. It comes from a late sixteenth-century Latin word *lucidus, lucere,* to shine, or *luc,* light. How interesting it is to meditate on the idea of my heart giving off the light of love!

I know that at this point in the book—the "heart" of the "heart book"—you, my reader would like me to tell you what my life looks like now that I am living more from the heart. Have I unlocked a sea of possibilities in my own life? Have I uncovered "hidden mysteries"? Do I find life exciting, as I had promised? Yes, in fact, I do. All of these things have happened. In recent months I have moved out of the role of an individual therapist into the role of a consultant to organizations. The world, as it were, has become my "client." This huge development in my life came suddenly and completely without expectation or forewarning. I was giving a talk at Green Acre, a Bahá'í conference center, about the ideas in my first book and also in this book when a gentleman from the audience realized that his prayer to have a psychologist join his team was being answered. He is a consultant to organizations and had been designing programs based on spiritual principles. He knew they were right, and he knew they worked, he just couldn't explain them to people from a psychological perspective. He needed this perspective in order to ground his work in science and enable it to grow and develop fully.

I had been praying too, as it turns out, for someone to help me with organizations. Again by chance, my work had taken me to large organizations for speaking engagements. Once the audiences began to understand my ideas, they immediately wanted to know how to apply them to their internal problems. I didn't have the answer.

So, at this moment, in this spiritual place, the answers to the two prayers came together in perfect harmony. We work together now in many different settings, our areas of expertise overlapping in an amazing complementary way.

Other things have happened too. To enumerate them would begin to seem like bragging. I have had a hard enough time being as "self-disclosing" as I have in this work so far. But I promise you that I am not just *talking* about the excitement and wonder of the spiritual journey. I am having the great fortune of *experiencing* it for myself. I am feeling a constant sense of gratitude all the time. It is a great way to live!

Meditation 7: Loving Kindness

In a lovely book called *Loving-Kindness: The Revolutionary Art of Happiness*, author Sharon Salzberg offers the following meditation, which is borrowed from the Buddhist tradition. She says classically there are four phrases used:

1. "May I be free from danger." Or alternatively "May I have safety" or "May I be free from fear."
2. "May I have mental happiness." Or alternatively "May I be happy" or "May I be peaceful" or "May I be liberated."

3. "May I have physical happiness." Or "May I be healthy" or "May I be healed." Or "May I make a friend of my body" or "May I embody my love and understanding."
4. "May I have ease of well-being." Or "May I live with ease" or "May loving-kindness manifest throughout my life" or "May I dwell in peace."[9]

Method

Sit comfortably. You can begin with five minutes of reflection of the good within you or your wish to be happy. Then choose three or four phrases that express what you most deeply wish for yourself, and repeat them over and over again. You can coordinate the phrases with the breath, if you wish, or simply have your mind rest in the phrases without a physical anchor. Feel free to experiment, and be creative. Without trying to force or demand a loving feeling, see if there are circumstances you can imagine yourself in where you can more readily experience friendship with yourself. Is it seeing yourself as a young child? One friend imagined himself sitting surrounded by all the most loving people he had ever heard of in the world, receiving their kindness and good wishes. For the first time, love for himself seemed to enter his heart.

Develop a gentle pacing with the phrases; there is no need to rush through them, or say them harshly. You are offering yourself a gift with each phrase. If your attention wanders, or if difficult feelings or memories arise, try to let go of them in the spirit of kindness, and begin again repeating the . . . phrases.[10]

After doing these meditations or others of your choosing for a few days, you may notice that your spiritual sight is sharpening. You may begin to notice the ways in which your life reflects your spiritual intentions. As you do so, you may find yourself moving into the next valley, the valley of Wonderment.

Journal Entry 29: Centering Prayer

For he hath burnt away the veils with his sighing, and unwrapped the shroudings with a single glance; with piercing sight he gazeth on the new creation; with lucid heart he graspeth subtle verities. This is sufficiently attested by: "And we have made thy sight sharp in this day."[11]

I have been reading a book called *Intimacy with God: An Introduction to Centering Prayer*, by Thomas Keating. Father Keating is a Cistercian monk and founder of the Centering Prayer movement. He is active with Contemplative Outreach, the organization he helped found to encourage contemplative prayer. He describes the spiritual journey of the contemplative monk in a language and manner that invites everyone to take part. He advocates a spiritual practice called "centering prayer," which I will describe in a moment. He explains that as the spiritual journey unfolds and levels of consciousness rise, it is possible to be healed of all our emotional pain and scars through the process of meditation, or, as he calls it, centering prayer.

Dr. Keating describes four "moments" in centering prayer. He begins by suggesting meditation on the sacred word as we are doing here. He then says it is important to rest in the awareness of God's presence in a state of contentment, peace, and interior silence as this valley describes. Then he says an "unloading" can occur in which

> . . . *a kind of psychological transference with God takes place. That is to say, God becomes the therapist in the psychoanalytic sense in which we look to the therapist for the trust and love that we did not feel we received as a child from an important other, such as a parent. The pain of rejection, which the emotions have stored in the unconscious and which is reactivated by every new rejection in life, is projected onto the therapist, who reflects back the acceptance that we did not adequately experience in childhood. This heals the emotional wounds in a way no amount of theological reflection can do.*[12]

In *It's Not Your Fault* I called the process "attunement." Father Keating says, "As a result of the deep rest of body, mind, and spirit, the defense mechanisms relax and the undigested emotional material of early life emerges from the unconscious at times in the form of a bombardment of thought or primitive emotions." Father Keating suggests that the prayerful one simply allow this process to unfold, allowing the emotions to let loose, to cry, or to feel whatever feelings come up. He says, "Emotions are energy. They can only be dissipated by acknowledging or articulating them."[13] He suggests that by staying with the process of contemplation, the mind and body and spirit will cleanse themselves as part of the natural healing process that is innate in all of us. The deep rest of contentment and confidence in God allows the natural healing to occur.

This type of experience is one that can and does occur "naturally" as part of advanced and long term spiritual practice. It is not fair to yourself to open a prayer book for the first time and say a few "short ones" and expect God to heal you instantly. I have had clients tell me at times, "prayer doesn't work." I believe that prayer does "work," but it takes time to form new patterns in your mind, body, and spirit. And the true state of your heart is key. If you are still enraged at your perpetrators, well, you have forgiveness work to do as part of your healing. If you carry a desire for revenge, no amount of meditation is going to "heal" you until you deal with this desire. Remember that love and hate cannot dwell in one heart.

I myself have experienced the healing force of prayer over and over again in my life. Without going into details, I promise you that I have every good reason to be totally "messed up"! I think I am pretty much OK in general (with lots of rough edges of course), but still, I am very clear and centered in my own foundation, which is and has always been the idea that I belong to God. No matter what happens in life, no matter what comes or goes, whether I am sick or healthy, rich or poor, this reliance on God remains as solid as rock. And so, here I am, typing away and sitting in amazement that I seem to have so much to say about all of this.

Meditation 8: Centering Prayer

The following guidelines for Centering Prayer are from Father Keating:

1. Choose a sacred word as the symbol of your intention to consent to God's presence and action within.
2. Sitting comfortably with eyes closed, settle briefly and silently introduce the sacred word as the symbol of your consent to God's presence and action within.
3. When you become aware of thoughts, return ever so gently to the sacred word.
4. At the end of the prayer period, remain in silence with eyes closed for a couple of minutes.

Stage Six: The Valley of Wonderment

At every moment he beholdeth a wondrous world,
a new creation, and goeth from astonishment to astonishment,
and is lost in awe at the works of the Lord of Oneness.
—BAHÁ'U'LLÁH, *THE SEVEN VALLEYS*

In the Valley of Wonderment, we are promised that we will go from "astonishment to astonishment." Part of the surprise is the amazingly graceful way life seems to flow when you are attuned to the spirit. Rather than do a lot of journaling in this valley, I would like to let the Seven Valleys speak to your heart directly. Now that you have been meditating and progressing spiritually, you may find you can understand and resonate to these passages in ways that would not have been possible earlier, before you began your spiritual practice in greater earnest.

I think these passages are some of the most beautiful and enlightening spiritual passages in any religious tradition that I have ever read. They contain so many profound facts about who I really am, my spiritual powers, and my place in the universe. For about the last ten years, I have been praying and meditating upon the phrase "Dost thou reckon thyself only a puny form when within thee the universe is folded?" In *Its Not Your Fault,* I told the story of a woman who was cured of a variety of emotional problems by hanging this powerful question on her refrigerator door and reading it many times each day. Her low self-esteem was eventually transformed, and she began to see herself as "important."

For me, dreams are key. I rely on my dreams. When I have an important decision to make, I arrive at the decision, then sleep on it to see what guidance may be revealed in the dream state. When I am writing and I get stuck, I take a nap. When I feel uneasy about something that I can't quite identify, I rest and sleep and often awaken with the intuition clarified. Sometimes I have wondered if the dream state takes us to reality and then we return here to the world of unreality, or delusion. What do you think?

Journal Entry 30: Wonderment

After journeying through the planes of pure contentment, the traveler cometh to the Valley of Wonderment and is tossed in the oceans of grandeur, and at every moment his wonder groweth. Now he seeth the shape of wealth as poverty itself, and the essence of freedom as sheer impotence. Now is he struck dumb with the beauty of the All-Glorious; again is he wearied out with his own life. How many a mystic tree hath this whirlwind of wonderment snatched by the roots, how many a soul hath it exhausted. For in this Valley the traveler is flung into confusion, albeit, in the eye of him who hath attained, such marvels are esteemed and well beloved. At every moment he beholdeth a wondrous world, a new creation, and goeth from astonishment to astonishment, and is lost in awe at the works of the Lord of Oneness.

Indeed, O Brother, if we ponder each created thing, we shall witness a myriad perfect wisdoms and learn a myriad new and wondrous truths. One of the created phenomena is the dream. Behold how many secrets are deposited therein, how many wisdoms treasured up, how many worlds concealed. Observe, how thou art asleep in a dwelling, and its doors are barred; on a sudden thou findest thyself in a far-off city, which thou enterest without moving thy feet or wearying thy body; without using thine eyes, thou seest; without taxing thine ears, thou hearest; without a tongue, thou speakest. And perchance when ten years are gone, thou wilt witness in the outer world the very things thou hast dreamed tonight.

Now there are many wisdoms to ponder in the dream, which none but the people of this Valley can comprehend in their true elements. First, what is this world, where without eye and ear and hand and tongue a man puts all of these to use? Second, how is it that in the outer world thou seest today the effect of a dream, when thou didst vision it in the world of sleep some ten years past? Consider the difference between these two worlds and the mysteries which they conceal, that thou mayest attain to divine confirmations and heavenly discoveries and enter the regions of holiness.

God, the Exalted, hath placed these signs in men, to the end that philosophers may not deny the mysteries of the life beyond nor belittle that which hath been promised them. For some hold to reason and deny whatever the reason comprehendeth not, and yet weak minds can never grasp the matters which we have related, but only the Supreme, Divine Intelligence can comprehend them:

How can feeble reason encompass the Qur'án,
Or the spider snare a phoenix in her web?

All these states are to be witnessed in the Valley of Wonderment, and the traveler at every moment seeketh for more, and is not wearied. Thus the Lord of the First and the Last in setting forth the grades of contemplation, and expressing wonderment hath said: "O Lord, increase my astonishment at Thee!"

Likewise, reflect upon the perfection of man's creation, and that all these planes and states are folded up and hidden away within him.

Dost thou reckon thyself only a puny form
When within thee the universe is folded?

Then we must labor to destroy the animal condition, till the meaning of humanity shall come to light.[1]

Questions: Wonderment

1. What does the question "Dost thou reckon thyself only a puny form when within thee the universe is folded?" mean to you in your own life?

2. Do you rely on your dreams? Have you ever done so? Have you ever ignored a dream and wished that you hadn't?

Journal Entry 31: Speaking Heart to Heart

In the previous valley, we are told that "only heart to heart can speak the bliss of mystic knowers."[2] I was astounded recently to experience this heart-to-heart communication for myself. A very dear friend of mine attended a conference at which I was presenting the ideas from this book for the first time. He amazed me at the end of the conference when he produced a poem he had written that seemed aimed directly at my heart. So many messages in his poem seemed to be just what my heart needed to hear. I have asked him to share this poem with you, my readers, and he has generously agreed to do so. I hope it speaks to your heart as it did to mine.

> *I sit before you.*
> *Enchanted, enthralled.*
> *Dazzled by your power,*
> *That of which you are but vaguely aware.*

Your awareness dulled because people like myself,
Have heaped the mud and detritus of our insecurities
Squarely upon your shoulders.

May God grant me the strength to break this cycle.
To resist, once and for all,
the temptation to add to your load.

And may He allow me to acknowledge the light,
still blazing brilliantly in your soul,
and to extend my hand in friendship,
that we may share in the heat and brilliance,
of a special bond longing to be discovered.

OVERCOME YOUR DOUBT!

For despite what some may have told you,
You are beautiful,
Just exactly as you are.

And despite what some may have called you,
You are worthy of love,
Just exactly as you are.

And despite what people may have done to you,
You are noble,
Just EXACTLY as you are.

I beseech the creator,
To give my words the power
To close the distance
That has come between us.

I long for our souls to become sewn together
with the golden threads of friendship and love.
And I pray that we may attract others, until
Every person, every creature, every plant and every rock,
Vibrate in unison.
Attuned with the mighty symphony of God.

—MIKE MARVIN

Stage Seven: The Valley of True Poverty and Absolute Nothingness

These journeys have no visible ending in the world of time,
but the severed wayfarer . . . may cross these seven stages
in seven steps, nay rather in seven breaths,
nay rather in a single breath, if God will and desire it.

—BAHÁ'U'LLÁH, *THE SEVEN VALLEYS*

I have tried to share a few thoughts about these spiritual planes. My musings are unimportant. I want to convey that these seemingly mystical and abstract ideas are very practical. They live in you and in your life.

It is also important to realize that I never "get there." I will never reach the end of my spiritual journey and just take a break. It's never time to just rest on my laurels, spiritually speaking. No, the cycles of the seven valleys go on, over and over again in my life. It is important to keep in mind that none of the valleys have definite beginning points or ending points. All of the valleys are really processes that enfold one another. The valleys can be seen as stages that we pass through again and again, just as we pass through the seasons of winter, spring, summer, and fall. Our spirits can easily lose their way in the winter, and then we must search for our Beloved as we did in the first valley, the Valley of Search. In the winter, the long winter, we need patience. In the spring, the Valley of Love, we ride the steed of pain as we plough the ground and suffer the labor of planting. Many of us can identify with the pain of love. In the summer, in the Valley of Knowledge, we see the fruits of our labors beginning to emerge, and the story of seeing the "end in the beginning" takes on many layers of significance. We cannot see the tree in the acorn without spiritual vision, faith, and the patience and labor of the earlier valleys. Then, in the fall, we see the things we have planted finally bearing fruit. In the fall, in the Valley of Unity, we truly see with our inner eyes. We are enlightened and rejoice in the harvest.

Ancient traditions from many cultures, including those of the Far East and those of Native Americans, speak of the four seasons and of the never-ending spiritual processes that continuously cycle on many planes and levels, bringing us ever more wisdom, ever deeper knowledge of our true spiritual core.

In *It's Not Your Fault* I spoke of four stages of the healing journey that can be compared to the four seasons. The healing journey begins in the winter when one is in pain and the scars are buried deep within. In the spring, when the healing work begins, one unearths the traumas and does the ploughing through old memories and old pain. As the traumas are worked through and healing begins, new potential is released. In the summer, new options begin to blossom and open up. And then in the fall, as the healing is more complete, the harvest time brings gratitude and an urge to be of service to others.

So, this four-season cycle of spiritual growth is archetypal and has deep roots within our psyche. It is not too hard for most of us to pick up the rhythm of this process and apply it to our own lives. This cycle of forgetfulness and remembrance is so central to spiritual growth, Bahá'ís remind themselves each day of all the things we have been talking about when we say our "obligatory" prayers. I quote the longest of the three daily prayers here. As I read it today, I was struck by the themes of belief, intention, attention, and action as they are reflected in this prayer. The directions for reciting the prayer include various body positions and gestures (actions). These actions do many things: they focus our attention, entrain our body/mind/spirit into a unified whole, and remind us of our relationship to the Creator as one of humbleness and gratitude, and many other spiritual blessings.

The prayer begins by immediately acknowledging belief in the Creator, "the Lord of all names and the Maker of the heavens," and it implores "the All-Glorious" "to make of my prayer a fire that will burn away the veils which have shut me out from Thy beauty, and a light that will lead me unto the ocean of Thy Presence."[1]

Then the prayer addresses the issue of intention and free will many times, at great length, in different words and passages. The prayer asks again and again for alignment of one's will to the will of the Creator. The language of the prayer urges God not to look upon "my hopes and my doings" but rather upon the will of God. It says, "Behold me standing ready to do Thy will and Thy desire" and implores God to "do with Thy servant as Thou willest and pleasest." It says, "Thine is the command at all times . . . and mine is resignation and willing submission to Thy will."[2]

The word "heart" appears many times in this prayer. For example, "Whatsoever is revealed by Thee is the desire of my heart and the beloved of my soul." The "lamentation" of the heart, or in other words, the pain and suffering of the heart are the result of sins and trespasses. This kind of separation from God melts hearts and souls. The following is one of my favorite passages from the prayer: "Too high art Thou for the praise of those who are nigh unto Thee to ascend unto the heaven of Thy nearness, or for the birds of the hearts of them who are devoted to Thee to attain to the door of Thy gate. I testify that Thou hast been sanctified above all attributes and holy above all names. No God is there but Thee, the Most Exalted, the All-Glorious."[3]

And so we find that each day is a whole new opportunity for spiritual growth. Each day is a springtime, a summer, a winter, and a fall. Each moment is a cycle, and each thought a season. As we turn to the light and love of God, we reflect this light to others and become illumined, enlightened, radiant beings—our true selves. From our hearts, the bounty of the hidden mysteries, talents, and potentialities pour out. We become instruments of the Divine Plan. Within this servitude, we are happy.

Journal Entry 32: Spiritual Existence is Immortality

I have been reading a passage about immortality that I find fascinating. It tells me that death is "absolutely unreal; it is only human imagination." It is interesting to me that my belief in death is directly related to my lack of spiritual progress. The passage tells me that when the veils are lifted from my inner eyes, when I see only with spiritual perception, I will witness "eternal light filling the world." I want to end the valley search with this passage that brings me great hope and peace. I find that I link it in my own mind to the passage about sleep and dreaming in the previous chapter. The passage about sleeping tells us that we can travel to distant lands and times and places each night. It educates us about what true existence is and reminds us that at least once a day, we all need our dose of true existence to keep on going. I wonder what it would be like to be as spiritually enlightened while awake! That is what they call it, don't they? Enlightenment. I hope you enjoy this passage as much as I did.

> According to divine philosophy, there are two important and universal conditions in the world of material phenomena; one which concerns life, the other concerning death; one relative to

existence, the other nonexistence; one manifest in composition, the other in decomposition. Some define existence as the expression of reality or being, and nonexistence as nonbeing, imagining that death is annihilation. This is a mistaken idea, for total annihilation is an impossibility. At most, composition is ever subject to decomposition or disintegration; that is to say, existence implies the grouping of material elements in a form or body, and nonexistence is simply the decomposing of these groupings. This is the law of creation in its endless forms and infinite variety of expression. Certain elements have formed the composite creature man. This composite association of the elements in the form of a human body is therefore subject to disintegration which we call death, but after disintegration the elements themselves persist unchanged. Therefore total annihilation is an impossibility, and existence can never become nonexistence. This would be equivalent to saying that light can become darkness, which is manifestly untrue and impossible. As existence can never become nonexistence, there is no death for man; nay, rather, man is everlasting and ever-living. The rational proof of this is that the atoms of the material elements are transferable from one form of existence to another, from one degree and kingdom to another, lower or higher. For example, an atom of the soil or dust of earth may traverse the kingdoms from mineral to man by successive incorporations into the bodies of the organisms of those kingdoms. At one time it enters into the formation of the mineral or rock; it is then absorbed by the vegetable kingdom and becomes a constituent of the body and fibre of a tree; again it is appropriated by the animal, and at a still later period is found in the body of man. Throughout these degrees of its traversing the kingdoms from one form of phenomenal being to another, it retains its atomic existence and is never annihilated nor relegated to nonexistence.

Nonexistence therefore is an expression applied to change of form, but this transformation can never be rightly considered annihilation, for the elements of composition are ever present and existent as we have seen in the journey of the atom through successive kingdoms, unimpaired; hence there is no death; life is everlasting. So to speak, when the atom entered into the composition of the tree, it died to the mineral kingdom, and when consumed by the animal, it died to the vegetable kingdom, and so on until its transference or transmutation into the kingdom of man; but throughout its traversing it was subject to transformation and not annihilation. Death therefore is applicable to a change or transference from one degree or condition to another. In the mineral realm there was a spirit of existence; in the world of plant life and organisms it reappeared as the vegetative spirit; thence it attained the animal spirit and finally aspired to the human spirit. These are degrees and changes but not obliteration; and this is a rational proof that man is everlasting, everliving. Therefore death is only a relative term implying change. For example, we will say that this light before me, having reappeared in another incandescent lamp, has died in the one and lives in the other. This is not death in reality. The perfections of the mineral are translated into the vegetable and from thence into the animal, the virtue always attaining a plus or superlative degree in the upward change. In each kingdom we find the same virtues manifesting themselves more fully, proving that the reality has been transferred from a lower to a higher form and kingdom of being. Therefore nonexistence is only relative and absolute nonexistence inconceivable. This rose in my hand will become disintegrated and its symmetry destroyed, but the elements of its composition remain changeless; nothing affects their elemental integrity. They cannot become nonexistent; they are simply transferred from one state to another.

Through his ignorance, man fears death; but the death he shrinks from is imaginary and absolutely unreal; it is only human imagination.

The bestowal and grace of God have quickened the realm of existence with life and being. For existence there is neither change nor transformation; existence is ever existence; it can never be translated into nonexistence. It is gradation; a degree below a higher degree is considered as nonexistence. This dust beneath our feet, as compared with our being is nonexistent. When the human body crumbles into dust we can say it has become nonexistent; therefore its dust in relation to living forms of human being is as nonexistent but in its own sphere it is existent, it has its mineral being. Therefore it is well proved that absolute nonexistence is impossible; it is only relative.

The purpose is this;—that the everlasting bestowal of God vouchsafed to man is never subject to corruption. Inasmuch as He has endowed the phenomenal world with being, it is impossible for that world to become nonbeing, for it is the very genesis of God; it is the realm of origination; it is a creational and not a subjective world, and the bounty descending upon it is continuous and permanent. Therefore man the highest creature of the phenomenal world is endowed with that continuous bounty bestowed by divine generosity without cessation. For instance, the rays of the sun are continuous, the heat of the sun emanates from it without cessation; no discontinuance of it is conceivable. Even so the bestowal of God is descending upon the world of humanity, never ceasing, continuous, forever. If we say that the bestowal of existence ceases or falters it is equivalent to saying that the sun can exist with cessation of its effulgence. Is this possible? Therefore the effulgences of existence are ever present and continuous.

The conception of annihilation is a factor in human degradation, a cause of human debasement and lowliness, a source of human fear and abjection. It has been conducive to the dispersion and weakening of human thought whereas the realization of existence and continuity has upraised man to sublimity of ideals, established the foundations of human progress and stimulated the development of heavenly virtues; therefore it behooves man to abandon thoughts of nonexistence and death which are absolutely imaginary and see himself ever living, everlasting in the divine purpose of his creation. He must turn away from ideas which degrade the human soul, so that day by day and hour by hour he may advance upward and higher to spiritual perception of the continuity of the human reality. If he dwells upon the thought of nonexistence he will become utterly incompetent; with weakened will-power his ambition for progress will be lessened and the acquisition of human virtues will cease.

Therefore you must thank God that He has bestowed upon you the blessing of life and existence in the human kingdom. Strive diligently to acquire virtues befitting your degree and sta-

tion. Be as lights of the world which cannot be hid and which have no setting in horizons of darkness. Ascend to the zenith of an existence which is never beclouded by the fears and forebodings of nonexistence. When man is not endowed with inner perception he is not informed of these important mysteries. The retina of outer vision though sensitive and delicate may nevertheless be a hindrance to the inner eye which alone can perceive. The bestowals of God which are manifest in all phenomenal life are sometimes hidden by intervening veils of mental and mortal vision which render man spiritually blind and incapable but when those scales are removed and the veils rent asunder, then the great signs of God will become visible and he will witness the eternal light filling the world. The bestowals of God are all and always manifest. The promises of heaven are ever present. The favors of God are all-surrounding but should the conscious eye of the soul of man remain veiled and darkened he will be led to deny these universal signs and remain deprived of these manifestations of divine bounty. Therefore we must endeavor with heart and soul in order that the veil covering the eye of inner vision may be removed, that we may behold the manifestations of the signs of God, discern His mysterious graces, and realize that material blessings as compared with spiritual bounties are as nothing. The spiritual blessings of God are greatest. When we were in the mineral kingdom, although endowed with certain gifts and powers, they were not to be compared with the blessings of the human kingdom. In the matrix of the mother we were the recipients of endowments and blessings of God, yet these were as nothing compared to the powers and graces bestowed upon us after birth into this human world. Likewise if we are born from the matrix of this physical and phenomenal environment into the freedom and loftiness of the spiritual life and vision, we shall consider this mortal existence and its blessings as worthless by comparison.[4]

Meditation 9:
Being Present and Accepting of What Is

A book by Eckhart Tolle called *The Power of Now: A Guide to Spiritual Enlightenment* has been a best seller. In it Mr. Tolle urges readers to leave the analytical mind and its false created self, the ego, behind. He urges readers to connect to the indestructible essence of our "being" which exists at all times with unceasing presence in this very moment. To become aware of our being in this moment without the delusional chatter and categorizing of the mind is to be in a kind of heaven. That is the message of this valley—the Valley of True Poverty and Absolute Nothingness. This "nothingness," this being—is ecstasy.

To be mindful is to be aware of the present moment, thus the title *The Power of Now*. He urges readers to come into awareness of the present and to have an attitude of acceptance. Acceptance is the key.

Mr. Tolle gives an exercise to invite his readers to connect with what he calls their "inner body" which he says "lies at the threshold between your form identity and your essence identity, your true nature. Never lose touch with it."[5] To get more in touch with your inner body, try the following exercise based on his advice:

Close your eyes. Become aware of your body. Feel the energy of your body. Feel your "aliveness." Do a body scan. Take your attention from the top of your head and breathe into each of the parts of your body. No specific formula or rigid sequence is necessary. When I do it with people it sometimes sounds something like this: If you are meditating alone at home, just follow your awareness through your body from the top of your head to the bottoms of your feet. Breathe "into" each part of your body. Your head, the top of your head, your cheeks, your jaw, your hair, your neck. Feel the weight of your head holding itself to your neck. Notice your neck connecting with your body, your shoulders, your chest, your back, your waist, your hips, your upper thighs, your legs, your feet, your arms, your wrists, your hands. Breathe, stay present, continue breathing and remaining present in your body for a time.

Journal Entry 33: True Poverty Is My Glory

After scaling the high summits of wonderment the wayfarer cometh to the Valley of True Poverty and Absolute Nothingness.

This station is the dying from self and the living in God, the being poor in self and rich in the Desired One. Poverty as here referred to signifieth being poor in the things of the created world, rich in the things of God's world. For when the true lover and devoted friend reacheth to the presence of the Beloved, the spar-

kling beauty of the Loved One and the fire of the lover's heart will kindle a blaze and burn away all veils and wrappings. Yea, all he hath, from heart to skin, will be set aflame, so that nothing will remain save the Friend. . . .

. . . He who hath attained this station is sanctified from all that pertaineth to the world. Wherefore, if those who have come to the sea of His presence are found to possess none of the limited things of this perishable world, whether it be outer wealth or personal opinions, it mattereth not. For whatever the creatures have is limited by their own limits, and whatever the True One hath is sanctified therefrom. . . .

This is the plane whereon the vestiges of all things are destroyed in the traveler, and on the horizon of eternity the Divine Face riseth out of the darkness, and the meaning of "All on earth shall pass away, but the face of thy Lord. . . ." is made manifest.[6]

Questions: True Poverty Is My Glory

1. Think about generosity in your own life. To give freely, without "strings attached" and to receive gratefully in love is a great joy. Think about that. Do you give freely or do you expect something in return when you give?

2. Look around your life. Look at your clothes, possessions, money, time, and talent. What could you give away for the good of others? How could you pursue "True Poverty" as a positive virtue?

3.   Think about astonishment. Make a list of all the things that you are grateful for. Is this list astonishing?

4.   What if you "gave away" your ego, your sense of self as separate from others?

Now we have moved through all seven of the stages of spiritual development. I hope you have found something in these pages that spoke to your heart and soul. In the next chapter, the conclusion, I will return to the ideas that got this book going and try to gain a deeper understanding and a perspective on all the things I have been learning.

Conclusion

I have presented a thesis, perhaps radical to modern ears, but grounded in timeless perennial wisdom: everything in our lives "proceeds from our own vision" from the inside out. To take responsibility for our inner life and the habits of our own mind and heart is the greatest responsibility of our lives. Free will operates throughout every single moment of every single day. It allows us to choose to turn our beliefs, our attention, and our actions to love and compassion or to selfish concerns. The choice is ours. No one can choose for us. No one can find our inner pathway for us. And no one can be blamed if we fail to become aware and choose consciously, purposefully, and carefully. The reality that unfolds in outer life is contingent upon the inner life of the soul.

The choices that the universe presents to us provide us with a proving ground for our souls. Everything that comes into our lives is, in this sense, a potential blessing. Everything that happens is an opportunity for our souls to learn. All trials, hardships, losses, setbacks, and failures are blessings, if we could but see with the eyes of God.

I think this statement may be pretty hard for some people to bear. What about my close friend who lost a son in a car accident on graduation night? What about my friend whose daughter contracted a debilitating nervous condition? What about my other friend whose husband has just died? What about war? How can any of these things be a blessing when they cause such tremendous grief and suffering? To say that grief and suffering are blessings sounds contradictory.

Remember Bahá'u'lláh's teaching story. He says that we are here to learn spiritual lessons, "period, end of it," as my husband says. Certainly, war is here to teach us that violence is destructive and not a way to solve problems. War itself is not a "blessing," but from war we can learn to do differently. Disease may not seem like a blessing, but from the courage and love of those who deal with disease, we see the Spirit at work. Tests and difficulties are just that—tests and difficulties. Some arise to show us the error of our ways, and some arise to deepen the spiritual soil of our hearts. Acceptance of tests and difficulties and looking at them with gratitude is a hallmark of spiritual development and the key to true and lasting happiness.

My Inner Reality Show

Most people seek happiness. Our culture tells us that happiness is to be found in the material world—bigger cars, nicer houses, designer clothes; it is all out there. Advertisers promise that these things will make us happy. And if these things do not satisfy us, how about power, prestige, and sexual attractiveness? Aren't these the real source of one's contentment? I have argued not only that they are not the source of happiness, but that they can be an impediment to happiness if they interfere with our ability to attune to God and others with love.

Magazines, television programs, books, lectures, and public instructional courses teach us various ways to set goals and make plans that will move us toward acquiring the external things we want and believe we need. Our attention is constantly drawn to a smorgasbord of possible external "fixes." Just yesterday as I was flipping through the channels on television, I was told how to make millions of dollars in real estate overnight, how to have my face altered with plastic surgery, how to lose lots of weight, and how to cook extravagant foods to impress my friends. I watched a makeover show that gave instructions about hair, cosmetics, and clothes selection. I watched a kitchen being made over, a garden being made over, and two people trading houses and making over each other's homes. I did not see one single program devoted to making over my inner life. I guess that is what I have tried to do. This has been my own inner "reality show." I have tried to be honest with you about my experiences while I have attempted to deepen spiritually. I have tried to record the truth about this process on a day-by-day, sometimes moment-by-moment basis.

I began my inward journey fascinated with dust and unable to sit still. The journal entries about the difficulties I encountered were completely real, completely honest. I did, on that first day, vacuum and avoid praying. I did, at the Chesapeake Bay, judge others based on my own prejudices, and while I was doing that I did believe that I was being holy and pious while in reality I was being selfish and egocentric. Needless to say, I have learned a great deal from this whole process.

In conversations with others, I often hear myself mentioning what I am learning. Just in the past few months I have noticed sentences such as these coming out of my mouth: "Ever since I started writing the book, I try not to judge." Or "Ever since I started studying the Seven Valleys, I have been trying to have more patience, because that's one of the tasks in the spiritual steps I am studying." "Ever since I started writing the book, I have more faith and see the 'end in the beginning' in things rather than feeling disappointed when things don't work out the way I had hoped." "Ever since I started the book, my heart seems more sensitive, and I am not as apt to make snap decisions with 'feeble reason' without checking in with my heart-wisdom first."

For me, this process of meditation, journaling, and sharing my spiritual journey with others has been one of surprise and discovery. The Bahá'í writings promise that within our own hearts "hidden mysteries" await. Undiscovered potential lies dormant. We are promised that to turn away from our outward senses and to open our inner senses is to find our true life of the heart. Bahá'u'lláh says, "And the splendor of that light is in the hearts, yet it is hidden under the veilings of sense and the conditions of this earth, even as a candle within a lantern of iron, and only when the lantern is removed doth the light of the candle shine out."[1] I began with that quotation, and though I know I have much, much more to learn, I now can say that I have actually experienced at least a taste of what this passage really means in my own life.

In the last few months I have had the opportunity to speak to audiences about the wisdom of the heart and how to tap into its hidden potential. I have taught these audiences meditation techniques and have had the privilege of actually meditating with the groups and talking with participants afterward about their experiences. Using various methods, I ask folks to turn their attention to their inward reality and begin to focus, breathe, and listen to the wisdom of their own hearts. Then, while in this state of quietude, the group sits in silence for ten to fifteen minutes or more. The sound of the silence is exquisite! Afterward, we talk about their experience while meditating. I am flooded with "thank yous." The looks on the faces of many of the audience members tell me that they have had a unique experience and that they are grateful for it. It is as if they feel we have visited their inner world together. Often, they do not say anything specific about their inner experience. Perhaps there are no words, or perhaps these experiences are too profoundly personal to be shared at that time. I only know that many tell me that this experience is valuable, something they need to use more and more in their own daily lives. Words that have been used to describe the meditation experience include "refreshing," "hopeful," "enlightening," and "very healing."

Thinking, Thinking, and Thinking

In the opening statement of the introduction, I promised a book that would teach you not to think. Recently, at one of the conferences at which I have spoken, I had an experience that caused me to realize I need to qualify that statement. After all, there are many kinds of thinking.

Thinking can mean so many different things. I am certainly not suggesting that we eliminate learning, reasoning, studying, investigating, problem solving, and all the productive activities of the mind that are sometimes called "thinking." Thinking is necessary to learn, to gather wisdom, and even to live from the heart. "Thinking," in the academic sense of the word, is a spiritual gift to humanity and an ongoing aspect of inner life. Indeed, the ability to balance spiritual insight with thought on many inner levels gives rise to what I am calling "the wisdom of the heart." The balance is a tricky one, though, as the following story illustrates.

At the conference I attended most recently, I was presenting ideas about the hidden potential of the heart and tapping into its wisdom. I spoke passionately about the heart as a wellspring of knowledge, and I urged the audience to abandon their reliance on thinking alone so that they might tap into this inner spiritual core. As I spoke, a woman began to interrupt me. I have come to think of her now as "the Interrupter."

Normally, when I give a presentation, my goal is to make an emotional connection with the audience. I try to attune to them, and I vigilantly monitor their nonverbal feedback to get a sense of how they are responding. If all goes well, a sort of magical moment emerges when the audience and I are one. In those moments I continue to speak on the topic at hand, but the words, the stories, the things that I say are not planned. They spring up, as it were, from the unique relationship I have formed with the audience.

A number of times, just as I was about to feel this bond become fruitful, the Interrupter would stand and even take the microphone to launch into what sounded for all the world like an academic lecture. Her tone was haughty and her manner arrogant. Her esoteric vocabulary gave rise to looks of confusion in the audience. The longer she spoke, the more agitated the audience became. I struggled to contain this intrusion by doing the things I usually do under such circumstances. I tried to listen, tried to join her in her ideas, tried to see if someone in the audience could paraphrase and restate her point more succinctly. Nothing worked. In fact, my efforts seemed to prolong her discourse.

Finally, I was able to silence her politely with a promise that in the afternoon, during the workshop portion of the conference, she would have time to discuss her ideas more fully. She sat down reluctantly but continued to be a source of distraction. She had positioned herself so far forward in the room that she was on a parallel with me, and she spent the rest of the time gazing out at the audience with a disgruntled look.

When the afternoon workshop time arrived, there she was again. Her demeanor remained hostile, and she again grabbed the microphone and launched into a confusing philosophical dissertation. More than one audience member politely said they didn't understand. Finally, a tall, distinguished elderly gentleman took control. He was clean-shaven, and bent with age. He said with an air of kind, patriarchal authority and a slight dismissing wave of his hand, "I think we need to move on. She isn't saying anything."

With that, a guided meditation began (through which the Interrupter coughed very loudly). Spiritual forces won out, and the meditation exercise seemed to be a success. Nevertheless, I remained disturbed by the interchange between this woman and me. Never before had such a thing happened to me in a conference or lecture situation.

The next morning I woke early and spent an hour in prayer and meditation. Then I went to a public area to find a quiet place to read. It was still before dawn. To my surprise, down the stairs and into my space came the Interrupter. "Good morning," she said. "I hoped I would find you here."

Since no one else appeared to be awake at this time, I must admit I found it surprising that she hoped to find me. But, trying to heed my own advice about everything being a blessing, I answered, "Come in, I was just reading, and I am happy to talk with you." This was true, since I thought that perhaps in one-on-one conversation I could finally come to understand her points.

Sure enough, we spoke for over two hours. She had many credentials, including advanced degrees from prestigious schools such as the one where she was now a professor. She proceeded to explain the distinction she was trying to make.

It all revolved around my advice not to think. She advised me that going to school, studying science, reading, in fact all intellectual pursuit, requires thinking. "Surely," she said, "you are not advocating the end to education?"

"No, of course not," I answered. "I am glad you brought my attention to this obvious omission and lack of clarification. Lack of clarity on this point can be very confusing." She shook her head crisply in the affirmative as if to say, "I won that one."

"And," she continued, "there is the kind of thinking that just 'arises' as the Buddhists speak about. This thinking is full of anxiety or worry or just enters as a distraction from prayer or connection with the spirit."

"Yes," I said, "that is the kind of thinking that we need to get rid of, if possible. That is the kind of thinking that is a distraction, an interference to spiritual concentration and attention." She again nodded in the affirmative, now confidently in charge. She was going for the kill now.

"And," she continued, her voice rising, "there is the kind of self-reflective thinking, the thinking in which you are able to stand outside of yourself and see yourself in the moment, doing what you are doing. This is what I meant when I said the polarity between subject and object collapses. In this moment, when this happens, you are able to be truthful with yourself, hold yourself accountable, see how you affect others and what you are really about."

"Yes," I agreed. She rolled back triumphantly in her chair and, pointing her index finger to the ceiling she proclaimed,

"*That* is what I was trying to say when *you kept interrupting me!*"

I remained calm and asked her, "When you were speaking yesterday in the group, were you in that state of self-reflection you talk about—seeing yourself in the moment, seeing what you were really about, what you were really trying to accomplish? Were you seeing your effect on me and on the audience?"

She paused for a long time as her face shifted this way and that, going suddenly from defiance to introspection, back to anger, and then finally to a steady state. She looked me in the eye. Now we had a connection. "No," she said, "I wasn't." It wasn't easy for her to admit this. I could tell from her facial expression.

"Well," I suggested, "would you be willing to do that now, to see yourself in that moment in your mind's eye?" Again there was a long pause. She closed her eyes and seemed to drift into a state of sleep of sorts, and when she opened her eyes again she said something that startled me. "I was the demon," she said. "My ego, the shadow side of me, it was in control. I didn't want to see that. I don't like seeing it now."

"So, the irony is, right now, you are *doing* what you were talking about yesterday. In fact, you and I were in complete agreement. You, however, wanted to talk *about* it, and I was trying to get the audience to *do it*, to *experience* it."

"Why do it that way?" she asked. "As long as they learn, what is the difference? Isn't it more efficient to just explain it?"

"No," I said. "Research on learning shows that people learn best from experience. How many times have you fallen asleep in a lecture? How about your students? Do they completely absorb everything you say? When we have an experience, our emotions are engaged. Emotion is closely tied with learning. Strong emotions tend to lead to long-lasting learning. Think about it some and apply it to your own life. I think you will see what I mean."

She looked at me now in a new way. Her mind seemed to be recalculating all that she had experienced from the day before, her angry insistence at being heard, her feeling of righteous indignation that I had interrupted her, her intention to make me wrong, and her belief that she was right. Her attention had been focused on ways to interrupt me, and her actions had been designed to discredit me. Evidently, these new realizations made her uncomfortable because she said, "Well, everyone has a shadow side. Everyone has to face their shadow in order to progress." I nodded affirmatively. Then she began another long, esoteric quote. Old habits die hard, I guess.

I paused and looked at her some more. I said, "Well, as my mother used to say, 'oyster/bannaner.'" She broke into a smile, aware that my nonsensical response said, in effect, "I am not going there. Academic one-upmanship is not what I am about." We shook hands, and we parted friends.

My interchange with the Interrupter was remarkable in that it brought together so many of the points I am trying to convey in this book. I began this discussion with the idea that states of consciousness fluctuate. I proposed the idea that when one raises one's state of consciousness through inner awareness and prayer, one moves toward love and compassion and toward "higher" states that are associated with unity and oneness with all mankind. I could see my Interrupter experiencing this right before my eyes. She began her discussion with me in one state of mind—feeling emotionally angry, ego involved (superior, arrogant), and then she decided to take an inner reality check. Then she saw a new reality. She saw herself as we saw her the previous day—as an impediment to the flow of love and unity. Her state of consciousness then shifted. This opened the door for her and me to connect. We looked each other in the eyes. We were on the same level of understanding. We became friends in this moment. We were both learning something. There was an exchange of powerful emotion that made this event something that both of us will remember. It was spiritual transformation in action.

I admire this woman, and I now consider her to be my friend. The transformation of our relationship rested first of all on her willingness to engage me one-on-one and secondly with her courage to face herself honestly. I don't think either of these things was easy for her to do, and both involve overcoming fear. Fear can paralyze the heart and send us running to cover ourselves with our own habitual defenses. Defenses are plentiful. Projection is always handy. We can see that this woman had projected her own desire to interrupt onto me, saying that I had interrupted her. And then we have denial. That is a tried and true defense. She denied that she was being egocentric and instead believed that she was only interested in truth.

This woman had defenses all right, but all of us have defenses of one kind or another. I think of them laid out on a big steam table, a cafeteria of ways to avoid inner truth. Let's see, in this chafing dish I see a main course of judgmentalism, perhaps with some side orders of anger and feelings of superiority? Or how about a dish of low self-esteem followed by side orders of jealousy and apathy? Then there is the old one-dish meal of feeling forever victimized by others accompanied by a desert of feeling therefore entitled to almost anything to rectify this perennial feeling of being a victim. I don't mean to be sarcastic, but let's face it, we all do this stuff. We all are the Interrupter at one time or another, aren't we?

But on this day, the Interrupter became the hero in her own story. Whatever her usual ways to avoid following her spirit might have been, she abandoned them all and courageously sought out my company, and it was early in the morning, too! She overcame her fear and her own veils and trauma points, all her old negative habits of heart, and she used her free will to make a choice to confront her inner reality by engaging in an authentic dialogue with me. She had other choices that would have had other consequences. For instance, she could have left the conference thinking very negatively about me, and if she had, I, too, would have left with a negative feeling toward her. I told her that without our "peace talk," if I had seen her again in a future audience, I would have reacted with fear and a desire to avoid her. "Fear," she said, "of the demon."

I give myself some credit, too, for trying to remain attuned to the Spirit while her assault was unfolding in front of the audience. I am glad I was able to remain open to hearing her. I explained to her that the emotional tone of her comments amounted to public shaming—certainly an experience of extreme negativity. Remember the Puritan punishment of the stocks, which forced a person to stand in public with their head and hands in a frame so that people could come along and jeer at them. Public shame is a powerful punishment. But I didn't react with shame to her comments because I could feel that her process was off. I could see that she didn't get it, and on that day, at least, I was clear about my own intention. This understanding kept me focused and helped me restrain my own ego defenses. Had it been some other day when I was less spiritually focused, I might have reacted defensively. That day, at least, my attention was focused on conveying love, and my actions flowed from this intention. To have deviated, to have reacted to her with anger, would have made me a hypocrite as well as a fool.

Another ironic fact about the Interrupter story occurred later in the afternoon, after my private talk with her. The patriarchal savior from the previous day who had finally quieted her approached me bent over on his cane and holding tightly to his wife's arm. His wife said that her husband wished to have a word with me because he had been worrying all night about his comment the previous day. "My goodness," I said. "I can't imagine why! You saved the day and helped me and the audience get back on track and stay in sync." He said, "You know, I have Alzheimer's disease." His wife nodded and whispered ever so softly so that he did not hear, "Dementia." I hugged him and reassured him that no one discerned anything but wisdom in his comment.

The flow of love between people is something palpable. It is unmistakable in its intention—the intention to connect, to join, to make everyone feel included and "a part of things." This love that flows from heart to heart knows no boundaries. Peoples of all cultures, all races, all levels of education, all states of health or ill health feel this love. My dear patriarch felt it and wanted more; he wanted whatever was interrupting this flow of love to stop. "Anything other than love," he said, "is really not about anything."

There is a beautiful statement from 'Abdu'l-Bahá that captures the essence of what I am trying to convey:

> The greatest gift of man is universal love—that magnet which renders existence eternal. It attracts realities and diffuses life with infinite joy. If this love penetrate the heart of man, all the forces of the universe will be realized in him, for it is a divine power which transports him to a divine station and he will make no progress until he is illumined thereby. Strive to increase the love-power of reality, to make your hearts greater centers of attraction and to create new ideals and relationships.
>
> . . . Create relationships that nothing can shake.[2]

Creating Relationships That Nothing Can Shake

I began this process with three questions in mind, questions that emanated from my first book, *It's Not Your Fault: How Healing Relationships Change Your Brain and Can Help You Overcome a Painful Past*. The first question concerned me and what has sustained me as I have attempted to help others heal from trauma. To answer this question, I tried to be as open and honest as I could be about what goes on within my own heart, and I tried to show the process and help you actually experience it yourself.

The second question was whether or not one can attune to the healing spiritual energies of the universe and access this energy directly without another living person as a conduit. I had talked about attunement in *It's Not Your Fault* as a way of healing. Attunement occurred between a mother and a baby or between two friends or relatives, or between a therapist and a client. The question was, can I attune to love in the universe itself? I hope you have seen through my journal entries that you can, and I hope you have done some of the exercises that may help you to experience these things for yourself.

The third question I posed was the issue of personal responsibility for one's own inner life regardless of outward circumstances. This is really the central idea of the book. Personal responsibility demands that we be aware of what we are really up to on a moment-by-moment basis. At this moment, what is the intention of my heart? Is it to love or is it to bring harm to someone, to prove someone wrong, to act out of greed, and so forth. At this moment, what am I paying attention to? Is it the loving forces of the universe, or is it my ego? At this moment, what am I choosing? How is my free will acting at this moment? Am I choosing to be aware of my inner truth? Am I choosing to act out of service to others? Am I choosing not to become preoccupied with material things? Am I choosing to try to grow spiritually? Or have I forgotten? And what about my actions? What do I see when I look at my actions? How do I spend my time? Trace your actions to their source in your heart. What treasure do you find there?

Belief, intention, attention, and action have proved to be good touchstones for me when I want to do an internal "reality check." Taking ownership of my inner reality, my true beliefs, and the intentions of my heart is a key to healing humanity's ills on many fronts of human endeavor. It seems that the majority of humankind, especially in the West, is in a massive state of denial that the inner intentions and beliefs of their own hearts are creating the world we share. It is important at this time in humanity's evolutionary process that these formerly unconscious dynamics of process-to-structure become fully conscious. Without conscious ownership, the forces of humanity's baser nature take over. Greed, lust for power, materialism, prejudices of many kinds, threaten the stability and longevity of our world. The answers cannot come from the old forms of political one-upmanship that have led us nearly to a world cataclysm. No, humanity needs a change of heart, and it needs it right away.

Perhaps our hardness of heart is a legacy of what Bahá'ís call the "old world order." The history of the last two thousand years has been a saga of war and struggles for power and control over resources. From the point of view of my thesis—that process creates structure—you can easily see from studying history that the greed and lust for power and material resources within the hearts of arrogant, foolish, and self-centered leaders of nations has repeatedly brought forth war and destruction. All of this violence has left its mark on the hearts of humanity. It has affected and continues to affect all of us. We are all on a healing journey of one form or another.

The Bahá'í Revelation tells us that humanity now has the spiritual capacity to become more fully aware and use the wisdom of their collective hearts to create a world of peace and unity. That is the point, the aim, and the process of the Bahá'í Revelation. The Bahá'í scriptures tell us that a new time, or "spiritual dispensation," is upon us. This is the time that humanity will unite and begin to experience what is referred to as the "Lesser Peace"—a time of bridge building and mutual cooperation and support among nations that will lay the groundwork for the prophesied "Most Great Peace."[3] We, all of us, you and I, are a part of building this peaceful world.

Peace begins within your own heart. Many have made this statement; many have even believed it—for a moment, for a time. But then we forget. Feeble reason takes over. Greed, lust, materialism, you name it, takes over. This pull between our spiritual nature and our lower material nature is not something that happens to *you* and not me. I cannot point my finger at you and ask you to get your act together. As the Bible says, I must look into my own eye and see the log blocking my vision instead of pointing out the speck in your eye. If my heart is busy judging you, I can be absolutely sure of one thing: I myself am completely spiritually off track.

Staying on Track

Getting on track and staying on track spiritually has been the subject of my journaling process. I hope you had a good laugh here and there. Let's face it; the ego doesn't give up easily. I began this process vacuuming up dust, with my spiritual life the size of a sprig of parsley on a turkey dinner. I began without being able to focus my attention or to calm myself down. I even had trouble sitting still! But I made a start, and my own inner wisdom told me to just try. The trying yielded lots of wisdom that continues to unfold for me each day. I discovered an access point and a method that works for me. Reading the inspired text and focusing on that while shifting my attention to my heart allowed me to "hear" my own inner voice. As I purposely "dethroned" my ego and its rattling, anxious noise, I was more and more able to hear the wise whisperings of my heart.

I have enjoyed sharing my thoughts this way. I have learned a great deal. I have learned things about myself, my "veils," my ego, and my forgetfulness of God. And I have also learned that I have not ever really forgotten God. I have lived the story of seeing the end in the beginning for as long as I can remember. Recently, I found an old Bible I used to read as a child, and many passages were underlined and the pages were curled from use. My spiritual journey began long ago, and I pray it will always and forever continue.

I have learned that journaling is a great form of meditation for me. I have found that the Seven Valleys is a bottomless wellspring of divine knowledge. The journal entries included in this book will not be my last, although I have no plans to share future entries in my personal journal. No, I think I have done what I set out to do with the journaling, which was to show those of you who read these pages both a method of self-reflection and to share a wonderful source of spiritual wisdom within Bahá'í writings. While I have quite literally fallen in love with the Seven Valleys, you need to find your own sources of spiritual wisdom and guidance. Meditation on any and all sacred scriptures is a pathway to deepening the Spirit. 'Abdu'l-Bahá tells us, "The Spirit breathing through the Holy Scriptures is food for all who hunger. God Who has given the revelation to His Prophets will surely give of His abundance daily bread to all those who ask Him faithfully."[4]

If a next book comes along, I am hoping it will focus on putting spiritual principles to work in the world within groups, communities, government organizations, businesses, and religious organizations.

It is impossible to really conclude a book like this. My own spiritual journey certainly does not end, and neither does yours. It cannot end. Bahá'u'lláh himself says, "These journeys have no visible ending in the world of time."[5] So, I cannot "conclude" or sum up this sharing of mine any better than Bahá'u'lláh has already summed it up for all of us. We come from the spiritual world, and we will return to the spiritual world where our journey will continue. The journey doesn't end.

Appendix

The Seven Valleys
In the Name of God, the Clement, the Merciful.

Praise be to God Who hath made being to come forth from nothingness; graven upon the tablet of man the secrets of preexistence; taught him from the mysteries of divine utterance that which he knew not; made him a Luminous Book unto those who believed and surrendered themselves; caused him to witness the creation of all things in this black and ruinous age, and to speak forth from the apex of eternity with a wondrous voice in the Excellent Temple*: to the end that every man may testify, in himself, by himself, in the station of the Manifestation of his Lord, that verily there is no God save Him, and that every man may thereby win his way to the summit of realities, until none shall contemplate anything whatsoever but that he shall see God therein.

---

* The Manifestation.

And I praise and glorify the first sea which hath branched from the ocean of the Divine Essence, and the first morn which hath glowed from the Horizon of Oneness, and the first sun which hath risen in the Heaven of Eternity, and the first fire which was lit from the Lamp of Preexistence in the lantern of singleness: He who was Aḥmad in the kingdom of the exalted ones, and Muḥammad amongst the concourse of the near ones, and Maḥmúd* in the realm of the sincere ones. ". . . by whichsoever (name) ye will, invoke Him: He hath most excellent names"† in the hearts of those who know. And upon His household and companions be abundant and abiding and eternal peace!

Further, we have harkened to what the nightingale of knowledge sang on the boughs of the tree of thy being, and learned what the dove of certitude cried on the branches of the bower of thy heart. Methinks I verily inhaled the pure fragrances of the garment of thy love, and attained thy very meeting from perusing thy letter. And since I noted thy mention of thy death in God, and thy life through Him, and thy love for the beloved of God and the Manifestations of His Names and the Dawning-Points of His Attributes—I therefore reveal unto thee sacred and resplendent tokens from the planes of glory, to attract thee into the court of holiness and nearness and beauty, and draw thee to a station wherein thou shalt see nothing in creation save the Face of thy Beloved One, the Honored, and behold all created things only as in the day wherein none hath a mention.

---

* Muḥammad, Aḥmad and Maḥmúd are names and titles of the Prophet, derived from the verb "to praise," "to exalt."
† Qur'án 17:110.

Of this hath the nightingale of oneness sung in the garden of Ghawth<u>í</u>yyih.* He saith: "And there shall appear upon the tablet of thine heart a writing of the subtle mysteries of 'Fear God and God will give you knowledge';† and the bird of thy soul shall recall the holy sanctuaries of preexistence and soar on the wings of longing in the heaven of 'walk the beaten paths of thy Lord,'‡ and gather the fruits of communion in the gardens of 'Then feed on every kind of fruit.'"§

By My life, O friend, wert thou to taste of these fruits, from the green garden of these blossoms which grow in the lands of knowledge, beside the orient lights of the Essence in the mirrors of names and attributes—yearning would seize the reins of patience and reserve from out thy hand, and make thy soul to shake with the flashing light, and draw thee from the earthly homeland to the first, heavenly abode in the Center of Realities, and lift thee to a plane wherein thou wouldst soar in the air even as thou walkest upon the earth, and move over the water as thou runnest on the land. Wherefore, may it rejoice Me, and thee, and whosoever mounteth into the heaven of knowledge, and whose heart is refreshed by this, that the wind of certitude hath blown over the garden of his being, from the Sheba of the All-Merciful.

Peace be upon him who followeth the Right Path!

---

* Sermon by 'Alí.
† Qur'án 2:282.
‡ Qur'án 16:71.
§ The holy Sanctuary at Mecca. Here the word means "goal."

And further: The stages that mark the wayfarer's journey from the abode of dust to the heavenly homeland are said to be seven. Some have called these Seven Valleys, and others, Seven Cities. And they say that until the wayfarer taketh leave of self, and traverseth these stages, he shall never reach to the ocean of nearness and union, nor drink of the peerless wine. The first is

The Valley of Search

The steed of this Valley is patience; without patience the wayfarer on this journey will reach nowhere and attain no goal. Nor should he ever be downhearted; if he strive for a hundred thousand years and yet fail to behold the beauty of the Friend, he should not falter. For those who seek the Ka'bih* of "for Us" rejoice in the tidings: "In Our ways will We guide them."† In their search, they have stoutly girded up the loins of service, and seek at every moment to journey from the plane of heedlessness into the realm of being. No bond shall hold them back, and no counsel shall deter them.

It is incumbent on these servants that they cleanse the heart— which is the wellspring of divine treasures—from every marking, and that they turn away from imitation, which is following the traces of their forefathers and sires, and shut the door of friendliness and enmity upon all the people of the earth.

In this journey the seeker reacheth a stage wherein he seeth all created things wandering distracted in search of the Friend. How many a

---

* The holy Sanctuary at Mecca. Here the word means "goal."
† Qur'án 29:69: "And whoso maketh efforts for Us, in Our ways will We guide them."

Jacob will he see, hunting after his Joseph; he will behold many a lover, hasting to seek the Beloved, he will witness a world of desiring ones searching after the One Desired. At every moment he findeth a weighty matter, in every hour he becometh aware of a mystery; for he hath taken his heart away from both worlds, and set out for the Ka'bih* of the Beloved. At every step, aid from the Invisible Realm will attend him and the heat of his search will grow.

One must judge of search by the standard of the Majnún of Love.† It is related that one day they came upon Majnún sifting the dust, and his tears flowing down. They said, "What doest thou?" He said, "I seek for Laylí." They cried, "Alas for thee! Laylí is of pure spirit, and thou seekest her in the dust!" He said, "I seek her everywhere; haply somewhere I shall find her."

Yea, although to the wise it be shameful to seek the Lord of Lords in the dust, yet this betokeneth intense ardor in searching. "Whoso seeketh out a thing with zeal shall find it."‡

The true seeker hunteth naught but the object of his quest, and the lover hath no desire save union with his beloved. Nor shall the seeker reach his goal unless he sacrifice all things. That is, whatever he hath seen, and heard, and understood, all must he set at naught, that he may enter the realm of the spirit, which is the City of God. Labor is needed, if we are to seek Him; ardor is needed, if we are to drink of

---

* The holy Sanctuary at Mecca. Here the word means "goal."
† Literally, Majnún means "insane." This is the title of the celebrated lover of ancient Persian and Arabian lore, whose beloved was Laylí, daughter of an Arabian prince. Symbolizing true human love bordering on the divine, the story has been made the theme of many a Persian romantic poem, particularly that of Niẓámí, written in 1188–1189 A.D.
‡ Arabian proverb.

the honey of reunion with Him; and if we taste of this cup, we shall cast away the world.

On this journey the traveler abideth in every land and dwelleth in every region. In every face, he seeketh the beauty of the Friend; in every country he looketh for the Beloved. He joineth every company, and seeketh fellowship with every soul, that haply in some mind he may uncover the secret of the Friend, or in some face he may behold the beauty of the Loved One.

And if, by the help of God, he findeth on this journey a trace of the traceless Friend, and inhaleth the fragrance of the long-lost Joseph from the heavenly messenger,* he shall straightway step into

The Valley of Love

and be dissolved in the fire of love. In this city the heaven of ecstasy is upraised and the world-illuming sun of yearning shineth, and the fire of love is ablaze; and when the fire of love is ablaze, it burneth to ashes the harvest of reason.

Now is the traveler unaware of himself, and of aught besides himself. He seeth neither ignorance nor knowledge, neither doubt nor certitude; he knoweth not the morn of guidance from the night of error. He fleeth both from unbelief and faith, and deadly poison is a balm to him. Wherefore 'Attár† saith:

For the infidel, error—for the faithful, faith;
For 'Attár's heart, an atom of Thy pain.

---

* Refer to the story of Joesph in the Qur'án and the Old Testament.
† Farídu'd-Dín 'Attár (ca. 1150–1230 A.D.), the great Persian Súfí poet.

The steed of this Valley is pain; and if there be no pain this journey will never end. In this station the lover hath no thought save the Beloved, and seeketh no refuge save the Friend. At every moment he offereth a hundred lives in the path of the Loved One, at every step he throweth a thousand heads at the feet of the Beloved.

O My Brother! Until thou enter the Egypt of love, thou shalt never come to the Joseph of the Beauty of the Friend; and until, like Jacob, thou forsake thine outward eyes, thou shalt never open the eye of thine inward being; and until thou burn with the fire of love, thou shalt never commune with the Lover of Longing.

A lover feareth nothing and no harm can come nigh him: Thou seest him chill in the fire and dry in the sea.

A lover is he who is chill in hell fire;
*A knower is he who is dry in the sea.**

Love accepteth no existence and wisheth no life: He seeth life in death, and in shame seeketh glory. To merit the madness of love, man must abound in sanity; to merit the bonds of the Friend, he must be full of spirit. Blessed the neck that is caught in His noose, happy the head that falleth on the dust in the pathway of His love. Wherefore, O friend, give up thy self that thou mayest find the Peerless One, pass by this mortal earth that thou mayest seek a home in the nest of heaven. Be as naught, if thou wouldst kindle the fire of being and be fit for the pathway of love.

---

* Persian mystic poem.

> *Love seizeth not upon a living soul,*
> *The falcon preyeth not on a dead mouse.**

Love setteth a world aflame at every turn, and he wasteth every land where he carrieth his banner. Being hath no existence in his kingdom; the wise wield no command within his realm. The leviathan of love swalloweth the master of reason and destroyeth the lord of knowledge. He drinketh the seven seas, but his heart's thirst is still unquenched, and he saith, "Is there yet any more?"† He shunneth himself and draweth away from all on earth.

> *Love's a stranger to earth and heaven too;*
> *In him are lunacies seventy-and-two.‡*

He hath bound a myriad victims in his fetters, wounded a myriad wise men with his arrow. Know that every redness in the world is from his anger, and every paleness in men's cheeks is from his poison. He yieldeth no remedy but death, he walketh not save in the valley of the shadow; yet sweeter than honey is his venom on the lover's lips, and fairer his destruction in the seeker's eyes than a hundred thousand lives.

---

* Persian mystic poem. Cf. *The Hidden Words,* No. 7, Arabic.
† Qur'án 50:29.
‡ Jalálu'd-Dín Rúmí (1207–1273 A.D.); The *Mathnaví*. Jalálu'd-Dín, called Mawláná ("our Master"), is the greatest of all Persian Ṣúfí poets, and founder of the Mawlaví "whirling" dervish order.

Wherefore must the veils of the satanic self be burned away at the fire of love, that the spirit may be purified and cleansed and thus may know the station of the Lord of the Worlds.

Kindle the fire of love and burn away all things,
*Then set thy foot into the land of the lovers.**

And if, confirmed by the Creator, the lover escapes from the claws of the eagle of love, he will enter

The Valley of Knowledge

and come out of doubt into certitude, and turn from the darkness of illusion to the guiding light of the fear of God. His inner eyes will open and he will privily converse with his Beloved; he will set ajar the gate of truth and piety, and shut the doors of vain imaginings. He in this station is content with the decree of God, and seeth war as peace, and findeth in death the secrets of everlasting life. With inward and outward eyes he witnesseth the mysteries of resurrection in the realms of creation and the souls of men, and with a pure heart apprehendeth the divine wisdom in the endless Manifestations of God. In the ocean he findeth a drop, in a drop he beholdeth the secrets of the sea.

Split the atom's heart, and lo!
Within it thou wilt find a sun.†

---

* From an ode by Bahá'u'lláh.
† Persian mystic poem.

The wayfarer in this Valley seeth in the fashionings of the True One nothing save clear providence, and at every moment saith: "No defect canst thou see in the creation of the God of Mercy: Repeat the gaze: Seest thou a single flaw?"* He beholdeth justice in injustice, and in justice, grace. In ignorance he findeth many a knowledge hidden, and in knowledge a myriad wisdoms manifest. He breaketh the cage of the body and the passions, and consorteth with the people of the immortal realm. He mounteth on the ladders of inner truth and hasteneth to the heaven of inner significance. He rideth in the ark of "we shall show them our signs in the regions and in themselves,"† and journeyeth over the sea of "until it become plain to them that (this Book) is the truth."‡ And if he meeteth with injustice he shall have patience, and if he cometh upon wrath he shall manifest love.

There was once a lover who had sighed for long years in separation from his beloved, and wasted in the fire of remoteness. From the rule of love, his heart was empty of patience, and his body weary of his spirit; he reckoned life without her as a mockery, and time consumed him away. How many a day he found no rest in longing for her; how many a night the pain of her kept him from sleep; his body was worn to a sigh, his heart's wound had turned him to a cry of sorrow. He had given a thousand lives for one taste of the cup of her presence, but it availed him not. The doctors knew no cure for him, and companions avoided his company; yea, physicians have no medicine for one sick of love, unless the favor of the beloved one deliver him.

---

* Qur'án 67:3.
† Qur'án 41:53.
‡ Qur'án 41:53.

At last, the tree of his longing yielded the fruit of despair, and the fire of his hope fell to ashes. Then one night he could live no more, and he went out of his house and made for the marketplace. On a sudden, a watchman followed after him. He broke into a run, with the watchman following; then other watchmen came together, and barred every passage to the weary one. And the wretched one cried from his heart, and ran here and there, and moaned to himself: "Surely this watchman is 'Izrá'íl, my angel of death, following so fast upon me; or he is a tyrant of men, seeking to harm me." His feet carried him on, the one bleeding with the arrow of love, and his heart lamented. Then he came to a garden wall, and with untold pain he scaled it, for it proved very high; and forgetting his life, he threw himself down to the garden.

And there he beheld his beloved with a lamp in her hand, searching for a ring she had lost. When the heart-surrendered lover looked on his ravishing love, he drew a great breath and raised up his hands in prayer, crying: "O God! Give Thou glory to the watchman, and riches and long life. For the watchman was Gabriel, guiding this poor one; or he was Isráfíl, bringing life to this wretched one!"

Indeed, his words were true, for he had found many a secret justice in this seeming tyranny of the watchman, and seen how many a mercy lay hid behind the veil. Out of wrath, the guard had led him who was athirst in love's desert to the sea of his loved one, and lit up the dark night of absence with the light of reunion. He had driven one who was afar, into the garden of nearness, had guided an ailing soul to the heart's physician.

Now if the lover could have looked ahead, he would have blessed the watchman at the start, and prayed on his behalf, and he would have seen that tyranny as justice; but since the end was veiled to him, he moaned and made his plaint in the beginning. Yet those who journey in the garden land of knowledge, because they see the end in the beginning, see peace in war and friendliness in anger.

Such is the state of the wayfarers in this Valley; but the people of the Valleys above this see the end and the beginning as one; nay, they see neither beginning nor end, and witness neither "first" nor "last."* Nay rather, the denizens of the undying city, who dwell in the green garden land, see not even "neither first nor last"; they fly from all that is first, and repulse all that is last. For these have passed over the worlds of names, and fled beyond the worlds of attributes as swift as lightning. Thus is it said: "Absolute Unity excludeth all attributes."† And they have made their dwelling-place in the shadow of the Essence.

Wherefore, relevant to this, Khájih 'Abdu'lláh‡—may God the Most High sanctify his beloved spirit—hath made a subtle point and spoken an eloquent word as to the meaning of "Guide Thou us on the straight path,"§ which is: "Show us the right way, that is, honor us with the love of Thine Essence, that we may be freed from turning toward ourselves and toward all else save Thee, and may become wholly Thine, and know only Thee, and see only Thee, and think of none save Thee."

---

* Qur'án 57:3.
† Saying attributed to 'Alí.
‡ Shaykh Abú Ismá'íl 'Abdu'lláh Anṣárí of Hirát (1006–1088 A.D.) Ṣúfí leader, descended from the Prophet's companion Abú Ayyúb. Chiefly known for his *Munáját* (Supplications) and *Rubá'íyyát* (Quatrains). Anṣár means the "Helpers" or companions of Muḥammad in Medina.
§ Qur'án 1:5.

Nay, these even mount above this station, wherefore it is said:

Love is a veil betwixt the lover and the loved one;
More than this I am not permitted to tell. *

At this hour the morn of knowledge hath arisen and the lamps of wayfaring and wandering are quenched.†
Veiled from this was Moses
Though all strength and light;
Then thou who hast no wings at all,
Attempt not flight.‡

If thou be a man of communion and prayer, soar up on the wings of assistance from Holy Souls, that thou mayest behold the mysteries of the Friend and attain to the lights of the Beloved. "Verily, we are from God and to Him shall we return."§

After passing through the Valley of knowledge, which is the last plane of limitation, the wayfarer cometh to

---

* Jalálu'd-Dín Rúmí (1207–1273 A.D.); The *Mathnaví*. Jalálu'd-Dín, called Mawláná ("our Master"), is the greatest of all Persian Ṣúfí poets, and founder of the Mawlaví "whirling" dervish order.

† This refers to the mystic wandering and search for truth guided by "Lights" or Ṣúfí leaders. Bahá'u'lláh here warns the mystics that the coming of the Divine Manifestation in His Day makes further search unnecessary, as it was said by 'Alí: "Quench the lamp when the sun hath risen"—the sun referring to the Manifestation of God in the New Day.

‡ Jalálu'd-Dín Rúmí (1207–1273 A.D.); The *Mathnaví*. Jalálu'd-Dín, called Mawláná ("our Master"), is the greatest of all Persian Ṣúfí poets, and founder of the Mawlaví "whirling" dervish order.

§ Qur'án 2:151.

The Valley of Unity

and drinketh from the cup of the Absolute, and gazeth on the Manifestations of Oneness. In this station he pierceth the veils of plurality, fleeth from the worlds of the flesh, and ascendeth into the heaven of singleness. With the ear of God he heareth, with the eye of God he beholdeth the mysteries of divine creation. He steppeth into the sanctuary of the Friend, and shareth as an intimate the pavilion of the Loved One. He stretcheth out the hand of truth from the sleeve of the Absolute; he revealeth the secrets of power. He seeth in himself neither name nor fame nor rank, but findeth his own praise in praising God. He beholdeth in his own name the name of God; to him, "all songs are from the King,"* and every melody from Him. He sitteth on the throne of "Say, all is from God,"† and taketh his rest on the carpet of "There is no power or might but in God."‡ He looketh on all things with the eye of oneness, and seeth the brilliant rays of the divine sun shining from the dawning-point of Essence alike on all created things, and the lights of singleness reflected over all creation.

It is clear to thine Eminence that all the variations which the wayfarer in the stages of his journey beholdeth in the realms of being, proceed from his own vision. We shall give an example of this, that its meaning may become fully clear: Consider the visible sun; although it shineth with one radiance upon all things, and at the behest of the

---

* Jalálu'd-Dín Rúmí (1207–1273 A.D.); The _Mathnaví_. Jalálu'd-Dín, called Mawláná ("our Master"), is the greatest of all Persian Ṣúfí poets, and founder of the Mawlaví "whirling" dervish order.
† Qur'án 4:80.
‡ Qur'án 18:37.

King of Manifestation bestoweth light on all creation, yet in each place it becometh manifest and sheddeth its bounty according to the potentialities of that place. For instance, in a mirror it reflecteth its own disk and shape, and this is due to the sensitivity of the mirror; in a crystal it maketh fire to appear, and in other things it showeth only the effect of its shining, but not its full disk. And yet, through that effect, by the command of the Creator, it traineth each thing according to the quality of that thing, as thou observest.

In like manner, colors become visible in every object according to the nature of that object. For instance, in a yellow globe, the rays shine yellow; in a white the rays are white; and in a red, the red rays are manifest. Then these variations are from the object, not from the shining light. And if a place be shut away from the light, as by walls or a roof, it will be entirely bereft of the splendor of the light, nor will the sun shine thereon.

Thus it is that certain invalid souls have confined the lands of knowledge within the wall of self and passion, and clouded them with ignorance and blindness, and have been veiled from the light of the mystic sun and the mysteries of the Eternal Beloved; they have strayed afar from the jewelled wisdom of the lucid Faith of the Lord of Messengers, have been shut out of the sanctuary of the All-Beauteous One, and banished from the Ka'bih* of splendor. Such is the worth of the people of this age!

And if a nightingale† soar upward from the clay of self and dwell in the rose bower of the heart, and in Arabian melodies and sweet

---

* The holy Sanctuary at Mecca. Here the word means "goal."
† This refers to Bahá'u'lláh's own Manifestation.

Íránian songs recount the mysteries of God—a single word of which quickeneth to fresh, new life the bodies of the dead, and bestoweth the Holy Spirit upon the moldering bones of this existence—thou wilt behold a thousand claws of envy, a myriad beaks of rancor hunting after Him and with all their power intent upon His death.

Yea, to the beetle a sweet fragrance seemeth foul, and to the man sick of a rheum a pleasant perfume is as naught. Wherefore, it hath been said for the guidance of the ignorant:

> *Cleanse thou the rheum from out thine head*
> *And breathe the breath of God instead.**

In sum, the differences in objects have now been made plain. Thus when the wayfarer gazeth only upon the place of appearance—that is, when he seeth only the many-colored globes—he beholdeth yellow and red and white; hence it is that conflict hath prevailed among the creatures, and a darksome dust from limited souls hath hid the world. And some do gaze upon the effulgence of the light; and some have drunk of the wine of oneness and these see nothing but the sun itself.

Thus, for that they move on these three differing planes, the understanding and the words of the wayfarers have differed; and hence the sign of conflict doth continually appear on earth. For some there are who dwell upon the plane of oneness and speak of that world, and some inhabit the realms of limitation, and some the grades of self,

---

* Jalálu'd-Dín Rúmí (1207–1273 A.D.); The *Mathnaví*. Jalálu'd-Dín, called Mawláná ("our Master"), is the greatest of all Persian Ṣúfí poets, and founder of the Mawlaví "whirling" dervish order.

while others are completely veiled. Thus do the ignorant people of the day, who have no portion of the radiance of Divine Beauty, make certain claims, and in every age and cycle inflict on the people of the sea of oneness what they themselves deserve. "Should God punish men for their perverse doings, He would not leave on earth a moving thing! But to an appointed term doth He respite them. . . ."*

O My Brother! A pure heart is as a mirror; cleanse it with the burnish of love and severance from all save God, that the true sun may shine within it and the eternal morning dawn. Then wilt thou clearly see the meaning of "Neither doth My earth nor My heaven contain Me, but the heart of My faithful servant containeth Me."† And thou wilt take up thy life in thine hand, and with infinite longing cast it before the new Beloved One.

Whensoever the Splendor of the King of Oneness settleth upon the throne of the heart and soul, His shining becometh visible in every limb and member. At that time the mystery of the famed tradition gleameth out of the darkness: "A servant is drawn unto Me in prayer until I answer him; and when I have answered him, I become the ear wherewith he heareth. . . ." For thus the Master of the house hath appeared within His home, and all the pillars of the dwelling are ashine with His light. And the action and effect of the light are from the Light-Giver; so it is that all move through Him and arise by His will. And this is that spring whereof the near ones drink, as it is said: "A fount whereof the near unto God shall drink. . . ."‡

---

* Qur'án 16:63.
† Ḥadíth, i.e. report of an action or utterance traditionally attributed to the Prophet Muḥammad or to one of the holy Imáms.
‡ Qur'án 83:28.

However, let none construe these utterances to be anthropomorphism, nor see in them the descent of the worlds of God into the grades of the creatures; nor should they lead thine Eminence to such assumptions. For God is, in His Essence, holy above ascent and descent, entrance and exit; He hath through all eternity been free of the attributes of human creatures, and ever will remain so. No man hath ever known Him; no soul hath ever found the pathway to His Being. Every mystic knower hath wandered far astray in the valley of the knowledge of Him; every saint hath lost his way in seeking to comprehend His Essence. Sanctified is He above the understanding of the wise; exalted is He above the knowledge of the knowing! The way is barred and to seek it is impiety; His proof is His signs; His being is His evidence.*

Wherefore, the lovers of the face of the Beloved have said: "O Thou, the One Whose Essence alone showeth the way to His Essence, and Who is sanctified above any likeness to His creatures."† How can utter nothingness gallop its steed in the field of preexistence, or a fleeting shadow reach to the everlasting sun? The Friend‡ hath said, "But for Thee, we had not known Thee," and the Beloved§ hath said, "nor attained Thy presence."

Yea, these mentionings that have been made of the grades of knowledge relate to the knowledge of the Manifestations of that Sun of Reality, which casteth Its light upon the Mirrors. And the splendor of

---

* Sermon by 'Alí.
† Ḥadíth, i.e. report of an action or utterance traditionally attributed to the Prophet Muḥammad or to one of the holy Imáms.
‡ The Prophet Muḥammad.
§ The Prophet Muḥammad.

that light is in the hearts, yet it is hidden under the veilings of sense and the conditions of this earth, even as a candle within a lantern of iron, and only when the lantern is removed doth the light of the candle shine out.

In like manner, when thou strippest the wrappings of illusion from off thine heart, the lights of oneness will be made manifest.

Then it is clear that even for the rays there is neither entrance nor exit—how much less for that Essence of Being and that longed-for Mystery. O My Brother, journey upon these planes in the spirit of search, not in blind imitation. A true wayfarer will not be kept back by the bludgeon of words nor debarred by the warning of allusions.

> *How shall a curtain part the lover and the loved one?*
> *Not Alexander's wall can separate them!* *

Secrets are many, but strangers are myriad. Volumes will not suffice to hold the mystery of the Beloved One, nor can it be exhausted in these pages, although it be no more than a word, no more than a sign. "Knowledge is a single point, but the ignorant have multiplied it."†

---

* Ḥáfiẓ: Shamsu'd-Dín Muḥammad, of Shíráz, died ca. 1389 A.D. One of the greatest of Persian poets.
† Hadíth, i.e. report of an action or utterance traditionally attributed to the Prophet Muḥammad or to one of the holy Imáms.

On this same basis, ponder likewise the differences among the worlds. Although the divine worlds be never ending, yet some refer to them as four: The world of time (*zamán*), which is the one that hath both a beginning and an end; the world of duration (*dahr*), which hath a beginning, but whose end is not revealed; the world of perpetuity (*sarmad*), whose beginning is not to be seen but which is known to have an end; and the world of eternity (*azal*), neither a beginning nor an end of which is visible. Although there are many differing statements as to these points, to recount them in detail would result in weariness. Thus, some have said that the world of perpetuity hath neither beginning nor end, and have named the world of eternity as the invisible, impregnable Empyrean. Others have called these the worlds of the Heavenly Court (*Láhút*), of the Empyrean Heaven (*Jabarút*), of the Kingdom of the Angels (*Malakút*), and of the mortal world (*Násút*).

The journeys in the pathway of love are reckoned as four: From the creatures to the True One; from the True One to the creatures; from the creatures to the creatures; from the True One to the True One.

There is many an utterance of the mystic seers and doctors of former times which I have not mentioned here, since I mislike the copious citation from sayings of the past; for quotation from the words of others proveth acquired learning, not the divine bestowal. Even so much as We have quoted here is out of deference to the wont of men and after the manner of the friends. Further, such matters are beyond the scope of this epistle. Our unwillingness to recount their sayings is not from pride, rather is it a manifestation of wisdom and a demonstration of grace.

> *If Khiḍr did wreck the vessel on the sea,*
> *Yet in this wrong there are a thousand rights.**

Otherwise, this Servant regardeth Himself as utterly lost and as nothing, even beside one of the beloved of God, how much less in the presence of His holy ones. Exalted be My Lord, the Supreme! Moreover, our aim is to recount the stages of the wayfarer's journey, not to set forth the conflicting utterances of the mystics.

Although a brief example hath been given concerning the beginning and ending of the relative world, the world of attributes, yet a second illustration is now added, that the full meaning may be manifest. For instance, let thine Eminence consider his own self; thou art first in relation to thy son, last in relation to thy father. In thine outward appearance, thou tellest of the appearance of power in the realms of divine creation; in thine inward being thou revealest the hidden mysteries which are the divine trust deposited within thee. And thus firstness and lastness, outwardness and inwardness are, in the sense referred to, true of thyself, that in these four states conferred upon thee thou shouldst comprehend the four divine states, and that the nightingale of thine heart on all the branches of the rosetree of existence, whether visible or concealed, should cry out: "He is the first and the last, the Seen and the Hidden. . . ."†

---

* Jalálu'd-Dín Rúmí (1207–1273 A.D.); The *Mathnaví*. Jalálu'd-Dín, called Mawláná ("our Master"), is the greatest of all Persian Ṣúfí poets, and founder of the Mawlaví "whirling" dervish order.
† Qur'án 57:3.

These statements are made in the sphere of that which is relative, because of the limitations of men. Otherwise, those personages who in a single step have passed over the world of the relative and the limited, and dwelt on the fair plane of the Absolute, and pitched their tent in the worlds of authority and command—have burned away these relativities with a single spark, and blotted out these words with a drop of dew. And they swim in the sea of the spirit, and soar in the holy air of light. Then what life have words, on such a plane, that "first" and "last" or other than these be seen or mentioned! In this realm, the first is the last itself, and the last is but the first.

In thy soul of love build thou a fire
*And burn all thoughts and words entire.**

O my friend, look upon thyself: Hadst thou not become a father nor begotten a son, neither wouldst thou have heard these sayings. Now forget them all, that thou mayest learn from the Master of Love in the schoolhouse of oneness, and return unto God, and forsake the inner land of unreality† for thy true station, and dwell within the shadow of the tree of knowledge.

O thou dear one! Impoverish thyself, that thou mayest enter the high court of riches; and humble thy body, that thou mayest drink

---

* Jalálu'd-Dín Rúmí (1207–1273 A.D.); The *Mathnaví*. Jalálu'd-Dín, called Mawláná ("our Master"), is the greatest of all Persian Ṣúfí poets, and founder of the Mawlaví "whirling" dervish order.
† This refers to the Ṣúfí idea of the inner plane, which compared to Revealed Truth is but unreal.

from the river of glory, and attain to the full meaning of the poems whereof thou hadst asked.

Thus it hath been made clear that these stages depend on the vision of the wayfarer. In every city he will behold a world, in every Valley reach a spring, in every meadow hear a song. But the falcon of the mystic heaven hath many a wondrous carol of the spirit in His breast, and the Persian bird keepeth in His soul many a sweet Arab melody; yet these are hidden, and hidden shall remain.

> *If I speak forth, many a mind will shatter,*
> *And if I write, many a pen will break.* *†

Peace be upon him who concludeth this exalted journey and followeth the True One by the lights of guidance.

And the wayfarer, after traversing the high planes of this supernal journey, entereth

The Valley of Contentment

In this Valley he feeleth the winds of divine contentment blowing from the plane of the spirit. He burneth away the veils of want, and with inward and outward eye, perceiveth within and without all things the day of: "God will compensate each one out of His abundance."‡

---

* Jalálu'd-Dín Rúmí (1207–1273 A.D.); The *Mathnaví*. Jalálu'd-Dín, called Mawláná ("our Master"), is the greatest of all Persian Ṣúfí poets, and founder of the Mawlaví "whirling" dervish order.
† This refers to Bahá'u'lláh Himself, Who had not yet declared His mission.
‡ Qur'án 4:129.

From sorrow he turneth to bliss, from anguish to joy. His grief and mourning yield to delight and rapture.

Although to outward view, the wayfarers in this Valley may dwell upon the dust, yet inwardly they are throned in the heights of mystic meaning; they eat of the endless bounties of inner significances, and drink of the delicate wines of the spirit.

The tongue faileth in describing these three Valleys, and speech falleth short. The pen steppeth not into this region, the ink leaveth only a blot. In these planes, the nightingale of the heart hath other songs and secrets, which make the heart to stir and the soul to clamor, but this mystery of inner meaning may be whispered only from heart to heart, confided only from breast to breast.

> *Only heart to heart can speak the bliss of mystic knowers;*
> *No messenger can tell it and no missive bear it.**

> *I am silent from weakness on many a matter,*
> *For my words could not reckon them and my speech would fall*
> *short.†*

O friend, till thou enter the garden of such mysteries, thou shalt never set lip to the undying wine of this Valley. And shouldst thou taste of it, thou wilt shield thine eyes from all things else, and drink of the wine of contentment; and thou wilt loose thyself from all things

---

* Háfiz: <u>Sh</u>amsu'd-Dín Muḥammad, of <u>Sh</u>íráz, died ca. 1389 A.D. One of the greatest of Persian poets.
† Arabian poem.

else, and bind thyself to Him, and throw thy life down in His path, and cast thy soul away. However, there is no other in this region that thou need forget: "There was God and there was naught beside Him."* For on this plane the traveler witnesseth the beauty of the Friend in everything. Even in fire, he seeth the face of the Beloved. He beholdeth in illusion the secret of reality, and readeth from the attributes the riddle of the Essence. For he hath burnt away the veils with his sighing, and unwrapped the shroudings with a single glance; with piercing sight he gazeth on the new creation; with lucid heart he graspeth subtle verities. This is sufficiently attested by: "And we have made thy sight sharp in this day."†

After journeying through the planes of pure contentment, the traveler cometh to

The Valley of Wonderment

and is tossed in the oceans of grandeur, and at every moment his wonder groweth. Now he seeth the shape of wealth as poverty itself, and the essence of freedom as sheer impotence. Now is he struck dumb with the beauty of the All-Glorious; again is he wearied out with his own life. How many a mystic tree hath this whirlwind of wonderment snatched by the roots, how many a soul hath it exhausted. For in this Valley the traveler is flung into confusion, albeit, in the eye of him who hath attained, such marvels are esteemed and well beloved. At every moment he beholdeth a wondrous world, a new creation, and

---

* Ḥadíth, i.e. report of an action or utterance traditionally attributed to the Prophet Muḥammad or to one of the holy Imáms.
† From Qur'án 50:21.

goeth from astonishment to astonishment, and is lost in awe at the works of the Lord of Oneness.

Indeed, O Brother, if we ponder each created thing, we shall witness a myriad perfect wisdoms and learn a myriad new and wondrous truths. One of the created phenomena is the dream. Behold how many secrets are deposited therein, how many wisdoms treasured up, how many worlds concealed. Observe, how thou art asleep in a dwelling, and its doors are barred; on a sudden thou findest thyself in a far-off city, which thou enterest without moving thy feet or wearying thy body; without using thine eyes, thou seest; without taxing thine ears, thou hearest; without a tongue, thou speakest. And perchance when ten years are gone, thou wilt witness in the outer world the very things thou hast dreamed tonight.

Now there are many wisdoms to ponder in the dream, which none but the people of this Valley can comprehend in their true elements. First, what is this world, where without eye and ear and hand and tongue a man puts all of these to use? Second, how is it that in the outer world thou seest today the effect of a dream, when thou didst vision it in the world of sleep some ten years past? Consider the difference between these two worlds and the mysteries which they conceal, that thou mayest attain to divine confirmations and heavenly discoveries and enter the regions of holiness.

God, the Exalted, hath placed these signs in men, to the end that philosophers may not deny the mysteries of the life beyond nor belittle that which hath been promised them. For some hold to reason and deny whatever the reason comprehendeth not, and yet weak minds can never grasp the matters which we have related, but only the Supreme, Divine Intelligence can comprehend them:

How can feeble reason encompass the Qur'án,
Or the spider snare a phoenix in her web? *

All these states are to be witnessed in the Valley of Wonderment, and the traveler at every moment seeketh for more, and is not wearied. Thus the Lord of the First and the Last in setting forth the grades of contemplation, and expressing wonderment hath said: "O Lord, increase my astonishment at Thee!"

Likewise, reflect upon the perfection of man's creation, and that all these planes and states are folded up and hidden away within him.

Dost thou reckon thyself only a puny form
When within thee the universe is folded? †

Then we must labor to destroy the animal condition, till the meaning of humanity shall come to light.

Thus, too, Luqmán, who had drunk from the wellspring of wisdom and tasted of the waters of mercy, in proving to his son Nathan the planes of resurrection and death, advanced the dream as an evidence and an example. We relate it here, that through this evanescent Servant a memory may endure of that youth of the school of Divine Unity, that elder of the art of instruction and the Absolute. He said: "O Son, if thou art able not to sleep, then thou art able not to die. And if thou art able not to waken after sleep, then thou shalt be able not to rise after death."

---

* Persian mystic poem.
† 'Alí.

O friend, the heart is the dwelling of eternal mysteries, make it not the home of fleeting fancies; waste not the treasure of thy precious life in employment with this swiftly passing world. Thou comest from the world of holiness—bind not thine heart to the earth; thou art a dweller in the court of nearness—choose not the homeland of the dust.

In sum, there is no end to the description of these stages, but because of the wrongs inflicted by the peoples of the earth, this Servant is in no mood to continue:

> *The tale is still unfinished and I have no heart for it—*
> *Then pray forgive me.**

The pen groaneth and the ink sheddeth tears, and the river† of the heart moveth in waves of blood. "Nothing can befall us but what God hath destined for us."‡ Peace be upon him who followeth the Right Path!

After scaling the high summits of wonderment the wayfarer cometh to

The Valley of True Poverty and Absolute Nothingness

This station is the dying from self and the living in God, the being poor in self and rich in the Desired One. Poverty as here referred to

---

* Jalálu'd-Dín Rúmí (1207–1273 A.D.); The *Ma<u>th</u>naví*. Jalálu'd-Dín, called Mawláná ("our Master"), is the greatest of all Persian Ṣúfí poets, and founder of the Mawlaví "whirling" dervish order.
† Literally Jayḥún, a river in Turkistán.
‡ Qur'án 9:51.

signifieth being poor in the things of the created world, rich in the things of God's world. For when the true lover and devoted friend reacheth to the presence of the Beloved, the sparkling beauty of the Loved One and the fire of the lover's heart will kindle a blaze and burn away all veils and wrappings. Yea, all he hath, from heart to skin, will be set aflame, so that nothing will remain save the Friend.

> *When the qualities of the Ancient of Days stood revealed,*
> *Then the qualities of earthly things did Moses burn away.**

He who hath attained this station is sanctified from all that pertaineth to the world. Wherefore, if those who have come to the sea of His presence are found to possess none of the limited things of this perishable world, whether it be outer wealth or personal opinions, it mattereth not. For whatever the creatures have is limited by their own limits, and whatever the True One hath is sanctified therefrom; this utterance must be deeply pondered that its purport may be clear. "Verily the righteous shall drink of a winecup tempered at the camphor fountain."† If the interpretation of "camphor" become known, the true intention will be evident. This state is that poverty of which it is said, "Poverty is My glory."‡ And of inward and outward poverty there is many a stage and many a meaning which I have not thought perti-

---

* Jalálu'd-Dín Rúmí (1207–1273 A.D.); The *Mathnaví*. Jalálu'd-Dín, called Mawláná ("our Master"), is the greatest of all Persian Ṣúfí poets, and founder of the Mawlaví "whirling" dervish order.
† Qur'án 76:5.
‡ Muḥammad.

nent to mention here; hence I have reserved these for another time, dependent on what God may desire and fate may seal.

This is the plane whereon the vestiges of all things are destroyed in the traveler, and on the horizon of eternity the Divine Face riseth out of the darkness, and the meaning of "All on the earth shall pass away, but the face of thy Lord. . . ."* is made manifest.

O My friend, listen with heart and soul to the songs of the spirit, and treasure them as thine own eyes. For the heavenly wisdoms, like the clouds of spring, will not rain down on the earth of men's hearts forever; and though the grace of the All-Bounteous One is never stilled and never ceasing, yet to each time and era a portion is allotted and a bounty set apart, this in a given measure. "And no one thing is there, but with Us are its storehouses; and We send it not down but in settled measure."† The cloud of the Loved One's mercy raineth only on the garden of the spirit, and bestoweth this bounty only in the season of spring. The other seasons have no share in this greatest grace, and barren lands no portion of this favor.

O Brother! Not every sea hath pearls; not every branch will flower, nor will the nightingale sing thereon. Then, ere the nightingale of the mystic paradise repair to the garden of God, and the rays of the heavenly morning return to the Sun of Truth—make thou an effort, that haply in this dustheap of the mortal world thou mayest catch a fragrance from the everlasting garden, and live forever in the shadow of the peoples of this city. And when thou hast attained this highest

---

* Qur'án 55:26, 27.
† Qur'án 15:21.

station and come to this mightiest plane, then shalt thou gaze on the Beloved, and forget all else.

The Beloved shineth on gate and wall
Without a veil, O men of vision.*

Now hast thou abandoned the drop of life and come to the sea of the Life-Bestower. This is the goal thou didst ask for; if it be God's will, thou wilt gain it.

In this city, even the veils of light are split asunder and vanish away. "His beauty hath no veiling save light, His face no covering save revelation."† How strange that while the Beloved is visible as the sun, yet the heedless still hunt after tinsel and base metal. Yea, the intensity of His revelation hath covered Him, and the fullness of His shining forth hath hidden Him.

Even as the sun, bright hath He shined,
But alas, He hath come to the town of the blind! ‡

In this Valley, the wayfarer leaveth behind him the stages of the "oneness of Being and Manifestation"§ and reacheth a oneness that is

---

* Farídu'd-Dín 'Aṭṭár (ca. 1150–1230 A.D.), the great Persian Ṣúfí poet.
† Ḥadíth, i.e. report of an action or utterance traditionally attributed to the Prophet Muḥammad or to one of the holy Imáms.
‡ Jalálu'd-Dín Rúmí (1207–1273 A.D.); The *Mathnaví*. Jalálu'd-Dín, called Mawláná ("our Master"), is the greatest of all Persian Ṣúfí poets, and founder of the Mawlaví "whirling" dervish order.
§ Pantheism, a Ṣúfí doctrine derived from the formula: "Only God exists; He is in all things, and all things are in Him."

sanctified above these two stations. Ecstasy alone can encompass this theme, not utterance nor argument; and whosoever hath dwelt at this stage of the journey, or caught a breath from this garden land, knoweth whereof We speak.

In all these journeys the traveler must stray not the breadth of a hair from the "Law," for this is indeed the secret of the "Path" and the fruit of the Tree of "Truth"; and in all these stages he must cling to the robe of obedience to the commandments, and hold fast to the cord of shunning all forbidden things, that he may be nourished from the cup of the Law and informed of the mysteries of Truth.*

If any of the utterances of this Servant may not be comprehended, or may lead to perturbation, the same must be inquired of again, that no doubt may linger, and the meaning be clear as the Face of the Beloved One shining from the "Glorious Station."†

These journeys have no visible ending in the world of time, but the severed wayfarer—if invisible confirmation descend upon him and the Guardian of the Cause assist him—may cross these seven stages in seven steps, nay rather in seven breaths, nay rather in a single breath, if God will and desire it. And this is of "His grace on such of His servants as He pleaseth."‡

---

* This refers to the three stages of Ṣúfí life: 1. *Shari'at,* or Religious Laws; 2. *Taríqat,* or the Path on which the mystic wayfarer journeys in search of the True One; this stage also includes anchoretism. 3. *Ḥaqíqat,* or the Truth which, to the Ṣúfí, is the goal of the journey through all three stages. Here Bahá'u'lláh teaches that, contrary to the belief of certain Ṣúfís who in their search for the Truth consider themselves above all law, obedience to the Laws of Religion is essential.

† *Maqám-i-Maḥmúd.* Qur'án 17:81.

‡ Qur'án 2:84.

They who soar in the heaven of singleness and reach to the sea of the Absolute, reckon this city—which is the station of life in God— as the furthermost state of mystic knowers, and the farthest home- land of the lovers. But to this evanescent One of the mystic ocean, this station is the first gate of the heart's citadel, that is, man's first entrance to the city of the heart; and the heart is endowed with four stages, which would be recounted should a kindred soul be found.

When the pen set to picturing this station,
*It broke in pieces and the page was torn.**

Salám!†

O My friend! Many a hound pursueth this gazelle of the desert of oneness; many a talon claweth at this thrush of the eternal garden. Pitiless ravens do lie in wait for this bird of the heavens of God, and the huntsman of envy stalketh this deer of the meadow of love.

O <u>Sh</u>ay<u>kh</u>! Make of thine effort a glass, perchance it may shelter this flame from the contrary winds; albeit this light doth long to be kindled in the lamp of the Lord, and to shine in the globe of the spirit. For the head raised up in the love of God will certainly fall by the sword, and the life that is kindled with longing will surely be sac- rificed, and the heart which remembereth the Loved One will surely brim with blood. How well is it said:

---

* Persian mystic poem.
† "Peace." This word is used in concluding a thesis.

Live free of love, for its very peace is anguish;
*Its beginning is pain, its end is death.**

Peace be upon him who followeth the Right Path!

* * * * * *

The thoughts thou hast expressed as to the interpretation of the common species of bird that is called in Persian *Gunjishk* (sparrow) were considered.† Thou appearest to be well-grounded in mystic truth. However, on every plane, to every letter a meaning is allotted which relateth to that plane. Indeed, the wayfarer findeth a secret in every name, a mystery in every letter. In one sense, these letters refer to holiness.

Káf or *Gáf* (K or G) referreth to *Kuffi* ("free"), that is: "Free thyself from that which thy passion desireth; then advance unto thy Lord."

Nún referreth to *Nazzih* ("purify"), that is: "Purify thyself from all else save Him, that thou mayest surrender thy life in His love."

Jím is *Jánib* ("draw back"), that is: "Draw back from the threshold of the True One if thou still possessest earthly attributes."

Shín is *Ushkur* ("thank")—"Thank thy Lord on His earth that He may bless thee in His heaven; albeit in the world of oneness, this heaven is the same as His earth."

---

* Arabian poem.
† The five letters comprising this word in Persian are: G, N, J, SH, K, that is, *Gáf, Nún, Jím, Shín, Káf.*

Káf referreth to *Kuffi,* that is: "Take off from thyself the wrappings of limitations, that thou mayest come to know what thou hast not known of the states of Sanctity."*

Wert thou to harken to the melodies of this mortal Bird,† then wouldst thou seek out the undying chalice and pass by every perishable cup.

Peace be upon those who walk in the Right Path!

---

* This and the foregoing quotations are from the teachings of Islám.
† This is a reference in the traditional Persian style to Bahá'u'lláh Himself.

Notes

Part One

Introduction
1. Bahá'u'lláh, *The Seven Valleys*, p. 33.
2. 'Abdu'l-Bahá, *Paris Talks*, no. 35.14.
3. Bahá'u'lláh, *Gleanings*, no. 117.1.
4. Bahá'u'lláh *Tablets of Bahá'u'lláh*, p. 173.

Belief, Intention, Attention, and Action
The epigraph for this chapter is from Bahá'u'lláh, *Gleanings*, no. 82.1
1. 'Abdu'l-Bahá, *Some Answered Questions*, p. 200.
2. See 'Abdu'l-Bahá, *Paris Talks*, no. 31.6
3. Bahá'u'lláh, *Gleanings*, no. 79.1.
4. 'Abdu'l-Bahá, *Paris Talks*, nos. 54.10–20.

The Seven Valleys as a Guide to Spiritual Development
1. Shoghi Effendi, *God Passes By*, p. 149.
2. Bahá'u'lláh, *The Seven Valleys*, p. 3.
3. Ibid., pp. 4–5.

Part Two

Stage 1: The Valley of Search

The epigraph for this chapter is from Bahá'u'lláh, *The Seven Valleys*, p. 5.

1. Bahá'u'lláh, *The Seven Valleys*, pp. 23–24.
2. 'Abdu'l-Bahá, *The Promulgation of Universal Peace*, p. 294.
3. Bahá'u'lláh, *The Seven Valleys*, p. 24.
4. Ibid., p. 33.
5. Ibid., p. 52.
6. Elena Mustakova-Possardt, *Critical Consciousness*, p. xiii.
7. Bahá'u'lláh, *The Seven Valleys*, p. 5.
8. Ibid., p. 5.
9. Ibid., p. 21.
10. Ibid., p. 4.
11. Ibid., p. 5.
12. See Matthew 5:15.
13. Bahá'u'lláh, *The Seven Valleys*, p. 5.
14. Ibid., p. 6.
15. Ibid., pp. 6–7.
16. Ibid., pp. 5–6.
17. Ibid., p. 5.
18. David Servan Schreiber, *The Instinct to Heal*, p. 36.
19. See 'Abdu'l-Bahá, *Paris Talks*, no. 6.7.
20. Bahá'u'lláh, *The Seven Valleys*, p. 5.
21. John Kabat-Zinn, *Full Catastrophe Living*, p. 59.

Stage 2: The Valley of Love

The epigraph for this chapter is from Bahá'u'lláh, *The Seven Valleys*, p. 8.

1. Bahá'u'lláh, *The Seven Valleys*, pp. 11, 10.

2. Ibid., pp. 7–8.
3. Ibid., p. 8.
4. Ibid.
5. Ibid., p. 9.
6. Ibid.
7. Ibid.
8. Ibid., pp. 9–10.
9. Ibid., p. 8.
10. Ibid., p. 18.
11. Bahá'u'lláh, The Hidden Words, Arabic no. 48.
12. 'Abdu'l-Bahá, Selections from the Writings of 'Abdu'l-Bahá, nos. 12.1, 12.3.
13. 'Abdu'l-Bahá, The Promulgation of Universal Peace, p. 294.

Stage 3: The Valley of Knowledge

The epigraph for this chapter is from Bahá'u'lláh, The Seven Valleys, p. 12.

1. Bahá'u'lláh, The Seven Valleys, p. 17.
2. Ibid., p. 12.
3. Ibid., p. 18.
4. Ibid., p. 13.
5. Ibid.
6. Ibid.
7. Ibid.
8. Ibid., pp. 13–14.
9. 'Abdu'l-Bahá, Selections from the Writings of 'Abdu'l-Bahá, no. 206.9.
10. Bahá'u'lláh, The Seven Valleys, p. 14.
11. Ibid.
12. Ibid., p. 14–15.
13. 'Abdu'l-Bahá, in Bahá'í Prayers, pp. 174–75.
14. Bahá'u'lláh, The Seven Valleys, pp. 16, 17.
15. Ibid.

Stage 4: The Valley of Unity

The epigraph for this chapter is from Bahá'u'lláh, *The Seven Valleys*, p. 18.

1. Bahá'u'lláh, *The Seven Valleys*, p. 20.
2. Ibid.
3. Ibid., p. 23.
4. Ibid., p. 18.
5. Ibid., pp. 18–19.
6. Ibid., p. 18.
7. Ibid., p. 21.
8. Ibid., p. 15.
9. Ibid., p. 19.
10. Ibid.
11. Ibid., pp. 20–21.
12. Ibid., pp. 21–22.
13. Bahá'u'lláh, *Gleanings*, no. 125.3.
14. Bahá'u'lláh, *The Seven Valleys*, pp. 22–24.

Stage 5: The Valley of Contentment

The epigraph for this chapter is from Bahá'u'lláh, *The Seven Valleys*, p. 30.

1. Bahá'u'lláh, *The Seven Valleys*, p. 30.
2. Ibid., pp. 28–29.
3. Ibid., p. 29.
4. Ibid., pp. 29–30.
5. Masaru Emoto, *The Hidden Messages in Water*, pp. 39–41.
6. Jeffery Satinover, *The Quantum Brain*, p. 174.
7. Albert Einstein, letter to D. Liplein, July 5, 1952, quoted in Jeffrey Satinover, The Quantum Brain, p. 127.
8. Bahá'u'lláh, *The Seven Valleys*, pp. 30–31.
9. Sharon Salzberg, *Loving-Kindness*, pp. 29–32.
10. Ibid.

11. Bahá'u'lláh, *The Seven Valleys,* p. 31.
12. Thomas Keating, *Intimacy with God,* p. 127.
13. Ibid.

Stage 6: The Valley of Wonderment

The epigraph for this chapter is from Bahá'u'lláh, *The Seven Valleys,* p. 32.

1. Bahá'u'lláh, *The Seven Valleys,* pp. 31–34.
2. Ibid., p. 30.

Stage 7: The Valley True Poverty and Absolute Nothingness

The epigraph for this chapter is from Bahá'u'lláh, *The Seven Valleys,* pp. 40–41.

1. Bahá'u'lláh, in *Bahá'í Prayers,* pp. 7–8.
2. Ibid., pp. 8, 12.
3. Ibid., pp. 8, 13, 12.
4. 'Abdu'l-Bahá, *The Promulgation of Universal Peace,* pp. 87–90.
5. Eckhart Tolle, *The Power of Now,* p. 113.
6. Bahá'u'lláh, *The Seven Valleys,* pp. 35–37.

Conclusion

1. Bahá'u'lláh, *The Seven Valleys,* p. 24.
2. 'Abdu'l-Bahá, *Divine Philosophy,* p. 111.
3. Shoghi Effendi, *The Promised Day Is Come,* p. 123.
4. 'Abdu'l-Bahá, *Paris Talks,* no. 16.10.
5. Bahá'u'lláh, *The Seven Valleys,* p. 40.

Appendix

Bahá'u'lláh, *The Seven Valleys,* pp. 1–43.

Bibliography

Works of Bahá'u'lláh

Gleanings from the Writings of Bahá'u'lláh. Translated by Shoghi Effendi. Wilmette, IL: Bahá'í Publishing, 2005.

The Hidden Words. Translated by Shoghi Effendi. Wilmette, IL: Bahá'í Publishing, 2002.

The Seven Valleys and the Four Valleys. New ed. Translated by Marzieh Gail and Ali-Kuli Khan. Wilmette, IL: Bahá'í Publishing Trust, 1991.

Tablets of Bahá'u'lláh revealed after the Kitáb-i-Aqdas. Compiled by the Research Department of the Universal House of Justice. Translated by Habib Taherzadeh et al. Wilmette, IL: Bahá'í Publishing Trust, 1988.

Works of 'Abdu'l-Bahá

Abdu'l-Baha on Divine Philosophy. Compiled by Elizabeth Fraser Chamberlain. Boston, MA: Tudor Press, 1918.

Paris Talks: Addresses Given by 'Abdu'l-Bahá in Paris in 1911. Wilmette, IL: Bahá'í Publishing, 2006.

The Promulgation of Universal Peace: Talks Delivered by 'Abdu'l-Bahá during His Visit to the United States and Canada in 1912. Compiled by Howard MacNutt. 2nd ed. Wilmette, IL: Bahá'í Publishing Trust, 1982.

Selections from the Writings of 'Abdu'l-Bahá. Compiled by the Research Department of the Universal House of Justice. Translated by a Committee at the Bahá'í World Center and Marzieh Gail. Wilmette, IL: Bahá'í Publishing Trust, 1997.

Some Answered Questions. Compiled and translated by Laura Clifford Barney. 1st pocket-size ed. Wilmette, IL: Bahá'í Publishing Trust, 1984.

Works of Shoghi Effendi

Advent of Divine Justice. 1st pocket-size ed. Wilmette, IL: Bahá'í Publishing Trust, 1990.

God Passes By. New ed. Wilmette, IL: Bahá'í Publishing Trust, 1974.

The Promised Day Is Come. 1st pocket-size ed. Wilmette, IL: Bahá'í Publishing Trust, 1996.

Compilations of Bahá'í Writings

Bahá'u'lláh, the Báb, and 'Abdu'l-Bahá. Bahá'í Prayers: A Selection of Prayers Revealed by Bahá'u'lláh, the Báb, and 'Abdu'l-Bahá. Wilmette, IL: Bahá'í Publishing Trust, 2002.

————. The Divine Art of Living: Selections from the Writings of Bahá'u'lláh, the Báb, and 'Abdu'l-Bahá. Compiled by Mabel Hyde Paine and revised by Anne Marie Scheffer. Wilmette, IL: Bahá'í Publishing, 2006.

[Bahá'u'lláh, 'Abdu'l-Bahá, and Shoghi Effendi.] Spiritual Foundations: Prayer, Meditation, and the Devotional Attitude: Extracts from the Writings of Bahá'u'lláh, 'Abdu'l-Bahá, and Shoghi Effendi. Wilmette, IL: Bahá'í Publishing Trust, 1980.

Other Works

['Abdu'l-Bahá and Auguste Forel]. *Auguste Forel and the Bahá'í Faith.* Translated by Hélène Neri. Commentary by Peter Mühlschlegel. Oxford: George Ronald, 1978.

Alcoholics Anonymous: The Story of how Many Thousands of Men and Women have Recovered from Alcoholism. New York: Alcoholics Anonymous World Services, Inc., 1976.

Allport, G. W. *Pattern and Growth in Personality.* New York: Holt, Rinehart, & Wilson, 1961.

Anscombe, G. E. M. *Intention.* Cambridge, MA: Harvard University Press, 1963.

Aristotle. *De Anima (On the Soul).* London, England: Penguin Books, 1986.

Armour, J. Andrew. "Neurocardiology: Anatomical and Functional Principles," The HeartMath Institue, http://www.heartmath.org/store/e-books/index.html.

Arntz, William and Betsy Chasse. *What the Bleep Do We Know!?* 20th Century Fox DVD, 2005. See http://whatthebleep.com/.

Austin, James H. *Zen and the Brain.* London, UK: The MIT press, 1998.

Bailey, Joseph V. *The Serenity Principle: Finding Inner Peace in Recovery.* San Francisco: Harper & Row, 1990.

Beck, A., Rush, J., Shaw, B., & Emery, G. *Cognitive Therapy.* New York: Guilford, 1979.

Beck, Don Edward and Christopher C. Cowan. *Spiral Dynamics: Mastering Values, Leadership, and Change.* Malden, MA: Blackwell Publishing, 1996.

Benson, Herbert. *Beyond the Relaxation Response: How to Harness the Healing Power of Your Personal Beliefs.* New York: Berkley Books, 1984.

———. *The Relaxation Response.* New York: Avon Books, 1975.

Benson, Herbert and Eileen Stuart. *The Wellness Book: The Comprehensive Guide to Maintaining Health and Treating Stress-Related Illness.* New York: Fireside, 1992.

Bergson, Henri. *Creative Evolution.* Mineola, New York: Dover Publications, 1998.

Bohm, David. *Thought as a System.* New York: Routledge, 1994.

———. *Wholeness and the Implicate Order.* London: Routledge, 1995.

Bowers, Kenneth E. *God Speaks Again: An Introduction to the Bahá'í Faith.* Wilmette, IL: Bahá'í Publishing, 2004.

Brown, Kevin. "'Abdu'l-Bahá's Response to the Doctrine of the Unity of Existence." *Journal of Bahá'í Studies.* Vol. 11, no ¾ (2001): pp. 1–29.

Bunns, David D. *The Feeling Good Handbook.* New York: Penguin Group, 1989.

Burger, Bruce. *Esoteric Anatomy: The Body as Consciousness.* Berkley, CA: North Atlantic Books, 1998.

Bushrui, Suheil. "The Age of Anxiety and the Century of Light: Twentieth Century Literature, the Poets Mission, and the Vision of World Unity." *Journal of Bahá'í studies,* vol. 13 no ½ (March–Dec. 2003): pp. 1–32.

———. "The 21st Hasan M. Balyuzi Memorial Lecture: The Opening of the Academic Mind: the Challenges Facing a Culture in Crisis." *Journal of Bahá'í studies,* vol 14, no ½ (March–June, 2004): pp. 1–38.

Capra, Fritjof. *The Web of Life: A New Scientific Understanding of Living Systems.* New York: Anchor Books, 1996.

Capra, Fritjof and David Steindi-Rast. *Belonging to the Universe: Explorations on the Frontiers of Science & Spirituality.* New York: HarperCollins, 1992.

Chalmers, David J. *The Conscious Mind: In Search of a Fundamental Theory.* New York: Oxford University Press, 1996.

Childre, Doc and Deborah Rozman. *Transforming Anger: The HeartMath Solution for Letting Go of Rage, Frustration, and Irritation.* Oakland, CA: New Harbinger Press, 2003.
———. Transforming Stress: *The HeartMath Solution for Relieving Worry, Fatigue, and Tension.* Oakland, CA: New Harbinger Press, 2005.

Combs, Allan. *The Radiance of Being: Complexity, Chaos and the Evolution of Consciousness.* St. Paul, MN: Paragon House, 1995.

Connelly, Dianne M. *All Sickness is Home Sickness.* Columbia, MD: Traditional Acupuncture Institute, 1993.
———. *Traditional acupuncture: The Law of the Five Elements.* Laurel, MD: Tai Sophia, 1994.

Csikszentmihalyi, Mihaly. *Flow: The Psychology of Optimal Experience.* New York: HarperCollins, 1990.
———. *The Evolving Self.* New York: HarperCollins, 1993.

Dalai Lama, Herbert Benson, Robert A. F. Thurmon, Daniel Goleman, Howard Gardner, et al. *Mind Science: An East-West Dialogue.* Boston: Wisdom Publications, 1991.

Dalai Lama and Howard C. Cutler, *The Art of Happiness: A Handbook for Living.* New York: Riverhead Books, 1998.

Dalai Lama. *The Good Heart: A Buddhist Perspective on the Teachings of Jesus.* Boston: Wisdom Publications, 1998.
———. *The Good Heart: Awakening the Mind, Lightening the Heart: Core Teachings of Tibetan Buddhism.* San Francisco: Harper, 1995.

Damasio, Antonio. *Descartes' Error: Emotion, Reason and the Human Brain.* New York: Quill, 1994.
———. *The Feeling of What Happens: Body and Emotion in the Making of Consciousness.* San Diego: Harcourt, 1999.

Duggan, Robert M. *Common Sense for the Healing Arts.* Laurel, Maryland: Tai Sophia Institute, 2003.

Emoto, Masaru. *The Hidden Messages in Water*. Hillsboro, OR: Beyond words, 2004.

Esslement, J. E. *Bahá'u'lláh and the New Era*. Wilmette, IL: Bahá'í Publishing, 2006.

Gillham, J. E., and M. E. P. Seligman. "Footsteps on the Road to a Positive Psychology." *Behaviour Research and Therapy*, 37 (1999) S163–S173.

Gibran, Kahlil. *The Prophet*. New York: Alfred A. Knopf, 1964.

Goldstein, Joseph and Jack Kornfield. *Seeking the Heart of Wisdom: The Path of Insight Meditation*. Boston: Shambhala, 1987.

Goleman, Daniel. *Destructive Emotions: How Can We Overcome Them?: A Scientific Dialogue with the Dalai Lama*. New York: Bantam Books, 2004.

———. *Emotional Intelligence*. New York: Bantam books, 1995.

———. *The Meditative Mind: The Varieties of Meditative Experience*. New York: G. P. Putnam's Sons, 1988.

Goswami, Amit. *The Self-Aware Universe: How Consciousness Creates the Material World*. New York: Penguin Putnam Inc., 1993.

Green, Brian. *The Elegant Universe: Superstrings, Hidden Dimensions, and the Quest for the Ultimate Theory*. New York: Vintage Books, 2000.

Hamer, Dean. *The God Gene: How Faith is Hard Wired Into Our Genes*. New York: Doubleday, 2004.

Hanh, Thich Nhat. *Touching Peace: Practicing the Art of Mindful Living*. Berkeley, California: Parallax Press, 1992.

Harman, Willis. *Global Mind Change*. San Francisco: Berrett-Koehler Publishers, 1998.

Hatcher, John S. *Close Connections: The Bridge between Spiritual and Physical Reality*. Wilmette, IL: Bahá'í Publishing, 2005.

Hatcher, John S. *The Purpose of Physical Reality.* Wilmette, IL: Bahá'í Publishing, 2006.

Hawkins, David R. *Power vs. Force: The Hidden Determinants of the Human Behavior.* Carlsbad, CA: Hay House, 2002.

Hawkins, David R. *Truth vs. Falsehood: How to Tell the Difference.* Toronto: Axial Publishing Company, 2005.

Hellaby, William and Madeline. *Prayer: A Bahá'í Approach.* Oxford: George Ronald, 1990.

Hobson, J. Allan. *Consciousness.* New York: Scientific American Library, 1999.

Hofman, David. *The Renewal of Civilization.* Oxford: George Ronald, 1994.

James, William. *Varieties of Religious Experience.* New York: Random House, 1902.

Johnson, Steven. *Mind Wide Open: Your Brain and the Neuroscience of Everyday Life.* New York: Scribner, 2004.

The Holy Bible, an Ecumenical Edition. New York: Collins, 1973.

Kabat-Zinn, Jon. *Full Catastrophe Living: Using the Wisdom of Your Body and Mind to Face Stress, and Pain, and Illness.* New York: Random House, 2005.

Keating, Thomas. *Intimacy with God.* New York: Crossroad, 2004.

Kirsch, I. and G. Sapirstein, "Listening to Prozac but Hearing Placebo: A Meta-Analysis of Antidepressant Medication." *Prevention & Treatment,* 1, article 0002a, posted June 26, 1998. http://journals.apa.org/prevention/volume1.

The Koran. Translated by N. J. Dawood. London: Penguin Books, 1999.

Lipton, Bruce. *The Biology of Belief.* Santa Rose, California: Mountain of love / elite books, 2005.

Maitland, Jeffery. *Spacious Body: Explorations in Somatic Ontology.* Berkeley, California: North Atlantic Books, 1995.

Maslow, A. *The Farthest Reaches of Human Nature.* New York: Viking, 1971.

McCraty, Rollin. "Heart-Brain Neurodynamic: The Making of Emotions," the HeartMath Institute, http://www.heartmath.org/store/e-books/index.html.

McCraty, Rollin, Mike Atkinson, Dana Tomasina. "The Science of the Heart: Exploring the Role of the Heart in Human Performance," The HeartMath Institute, http://www.heartmath.org/store/e-books/index.html.

McGraw, Patricia Romano. *It's Not Your Fault: How Healing Relationships Change Your Brain & Can Help You Overcome a Painful Past.* Wilmette, IL: Bahá'í publishing, 2004.

Mclean, J. A. *Dimensions in Spirituality.* Oxford: George Ronald, 1994.

McTaggart, Lynne. *The Field: The Quest for the Secret Force of the Universe.* New York: Quill, 2002.

Mind & Life Institute, http://mindandlife.org/.

Momen, Wendi. *Meditation.* Oxford: George Ronald, 1999.

Mustakova-Possardt, Elena. *Critical Consciousness: A Study of Morality in Global Historical Context.* Westport, CT: Praeger, 2003.

Myers, D. G. "The Funds, Friends, and Faith of Happy People." *American Psychologist,* 55, (2002): pp. 56–67.

Newberg, Andrew, Eugene D'Aquili, Vince Rause. *Why God Won't Go Away: Brain Science & the Biology of Belief.* New York: Ballantine Books, 2001.

Pearce, Joseph Chilton. *The Biology of Transcendence: A Blueprint of the Human Spirit.* Rochester, Vermont: Park Street Press, 2002.

Pert, Candace B. *Molecules of Emotion: The Science behind Mind-Body Medicine*. New York: Touchstone, 1997.

Peterson, C. "The Future of Optimism." *American Psychologist*, 55, (2000): pp. 44–55.

Satinover, Jeffry. *The Quantum Brain: The Search for Freedom and the Next Generation of Man*. New York: John Wiley & Sons, 2001.

Salzberg, Sharon. *Loving Kindness: The Revolutionary Art of Happiness*. Boston: Shambhala, 2002.

Schore, Allan N. *Affect Regulation and the Origin of the Self: The Neurobiology of Emotional Development*. Hillsdale, New Jersey: Lawrence Erlbaum Associates, 1994.

Schwartz, B. "Self-Determination: The Tyranny of Freedom." *American Psychologist*, 55, (2000): pp. 79–88.

Seligman, M. *What You Can Change and What You Can't*. New York: Knopf, 1994.

Seligman, M.E.P. "The Effectiveness of Psychotherapy: The Consumer Reports Study." *American Psychologist*, 50 (1995): pp. 965–74.

Servan-Schreiber, David. *The Instinct to Heal: Curing Stress, Anxiety, and Depression Without Drugs and Without Talk Therapy*. Emmaus, PA: 2004.

Sheldrake, Rubert. *A New Science of Life: The Hypothesis of Morphic Resonance*. Rochester, Vermont: Park Street Press, 1995.

Sperry, Len and Edward P. Shafranske. *Spiritually Oriented Psychotherapy*. Washington, D.C.: American Psychological Association, 2005.

Sullivan, John. Living Large: Transformative Work at the Intersection of Ethics and Spirituality. Laurel, MD: Tai Sophia Institute, 2004.

Templeton, Sir John. *Wisdom from World Religions: Pathways Toward Heaven on Earth*. Philadelphia: Templeton Foundation Press, 2002.

Thich Nhat Hanh. *Touching Peace: Practicing the Art of Mindful Living*. Berkley, CA: Parallax Press, 1992.

Tiller, William A., Walter E. Dibble, Michael J. Kohane. *Conscious Acts of Creation: The Emergence of a New Physics*. Walnut Creek, CA: Pavion Publishing, 2001.

Tolle, Eckhart. *The Power of Now: A Guide to Spiritual Enlightenment*. Novato, CA: Namaste Publishing & New World Library, 1999.

Townshend, George. *The Heart of the Gospel*. Oxford: George Ronald, 1995.

Trine, Ralph Waldo. *Every Living Creature: Heart-Training Through the Animal World*. New York: Dodge Publishing Company, 1899.

Warren, Rick. *The Purpose Driven Life: What on Earth am I Here For?* Grand Rapids, MI: Zondervan, 2002.

Weil, Andrew. *Spontaneous Healing*. New York: Alfred A. Knopf, 1995.

Weil, Henry A. *Closer Than Your Life-Vein: An Insight Into the Wonders of Spiritual Fulfillment*. Alaska: National Spiritual Assembly of the Bahá'ís of Alaska, 1978.

————. *Drops from the Ocean*. New Delhi, India: Bahá'í Publishing Trust, 1987.

Wilber, Ken. *Integral Psychology: Consciousness, Spirit, Psychology, Therapy*. Boston: Shambhala, 2000.

————. *The Spectrum of Consciousness*. Wheaton, IL: Quest Books, 1993.

Williamson, Marianne. *A Return to Love: Reflections on the Principles of a Course in Miracles*. New York: HarperCollins, 1992.

Wolf, Fred Alan. *Matter Into Feeling: A New Alchemy of Science and Spirit*. Portsmouth, New Hampshire: Moment Point Press, 2002.

Zukav, Gary. *The Dancing Wu Li Masters: an Overview of the New Physics.* New York: Bantam Books, 1979.
———. *The Heart of the Soul: Emotional Awareness.* New York: Simon & Schuster Source, 2001.
———. *The Seat of the Soul.* New York: Fireside, 1989.
Zukav, Gary and Linda Francis. *The Mind of the Soul.* New York: Free Press, 2003.

Index

Other Books Available from Bahá'í Publishing

The Prisoner and the Kings:
How One Man Changed the Course of History
William Sears
$12.00 U.S. / $15.00 CAN
Trade Paper
1-931847-41-X
978-1-931847-41-4

The Prisoner and the Kings: How One Man Changed the Course of History tells the story of one of the greatest sagas of modern times. Between 1867 and 1873 a solitary prisoner in a Turkish penal colony wrote a series of letters to the kings and emperors of the day, predicting with amazing accuracy the course of modern history: the fall of several nations, the overthrow of certain individual monarchs, the decline of specific religious institutions, the rise of communism, and the threat of nuclear weapons. The prisoner was Bahá'u'lláh, Prophet and Founder of the Bahá'í Faith, one of the most remarkable figures in this or any age. What was the secret behind this handful of amazing communications? What was the source of the prisoner's knowledge? And what did the letters have to say about the future of humanity in the twenty-first century? The answers are here, in this riveting historical account of a most unusual prisoner and His world-changing letters to religious and secular leaders.

Peace: More than an End to War
Foreword by Peter Khan
$18.00 U.S. / $21.00 CAN
Trade Paper
1-931847-39-8
978-1-931847-39-1

The horrors of innumerable conflicts currently blazing throughout the globe would seem to indicate that world peace is nothing more than a childish fantasy. But members of the Bahá'í Faith believe that the future is filled with hope and promise, for the Bahá'í writings state unequivocally that world peace is not only possible, it's inevitable.

How can this be? The selections from the Bahá'í writings in this compilation spell out how world peace can be achieved. They explain that humanity is in a transition from adolescence to adulthood, that the spiritual roots of peace must be identified, and that the barriers to peace—racism, extremes of wealth and poverty, the denial of the equality of men and women, and unbridled nationalism and religious strife—must be eliminated in order to lay the groundwork for true and lasting peace. The book discusses the essential Bahá'í principles of the oneness of humanity and the oneness of religion as being critical to the creation of a true and lasting peace.

Peace: More than an End to War is a blueprint both for the peace of the individual and the peace of our global society. This timely compilation can bring comfort to the world-weary souls who pause to explore the wisdom in its pages.

One World, One People:
How Globalization Is Shaping Our Future
Gregory C. Dahl
$15.00 U.S. / $18.00 CAN
Trade Paper
1-931847-35-5
978-1-931847-35-3

In the midst of accelerating change, our world seems to be in crisis. It is widely accepted that our planet is rapidly becoming smaller and more interconnected, while the policies, ideas, and institutions of the past are weakening in the face of new challenges. In *One World, One People,* author Gregory C. Dahl offers a penetrating look at the questions surrounding globalization not only in economics but in all aspects of human life. Surveying the past century's developments in technology, ideology, and politics, he shows how the current world situation arose from forces that are gradually contracting the planet and its societies. Drawing on his many years of experience working for the International Monetary Fund and from insights provided by the Bahá'í Faith, Dahl offers evidence of the inevitable path toward world unity. His critical examination of history, political influences, and implications of global trends suggests a promising future for all of humankind.

Gems from the World's Great Scriptures
Compiled and introduced by David Jurney
$12.00 U.S. / $15.00 CAN
Trade Paper
1-931847-43-6
978-1-931847-43-8

Have you ever wondered what other religions teach about creation, prayer, faith? *Gems from the World's Great Scriptures* answers these questions and more in a beautifully arranged selection of scriptures taken from six religions: Hinduism, Buddhism, Judaism, Christianity, Islam, and the Bahá'í Faith. Each chapter covers a different topic and offers insight and inspiration on a theme gleaned from the sacred writings of different faiths. What emerges is a unique love story—the story of God's love and guidance for all humankind.

Gems from the World's Great Scriptures is a valuable collection for anyone interested in connecting to the spirit of words that have offered hope and solace to people since the beginning of history.

Bahá'u'lláh and the New Era:
An Introduction to the Bahá'í Faith
J. E. Esslemont
Trade Paper
$14.00 U.S. / $17.00 CAN
1-931847-27-4
978-1-931847-33-9

Bahá'u'lláh and the New Era shines as the most widely known and enduring textbook of the Bahá'í Faith. In this compact work, Esslemont comprehensively yet succinctly sets forth the teachings of Bahá'u'lláh, the Prophet and Founder of the Bahá'í Faith. He outlines the religion's early history, explains its theology, incorporates extracts from Bahá'í scripture, and provides information on Bahá'í spiritual practices. This is an excellent introduction to the Bahá'í Faith and the worldwide Bahá'í community, whose members represent what may well be the most ethnically and culturally diverse association of people in the world. The book, translated into some sixty languages since its initial publication in 1923, is a must-read for those interested in the study of the world's great religions.

Faith, Physics, and Psychology:
Rethinking Society and the Human Spirit
John Fitzgerald Medina
$17.00 U.S. / $20.00 CAN
Trade Paper
1-931847-30-4
978-1-931847-30-8

In *Faith, Physics, and Psychology,* John Medina explores new developments in three different but complementary movements—physics, psychology, and religion—that reflect a new understanding of what it means to be human. Written in the style of Fritjof Capra's *The Turning Point: Science, Society, and the Rising Culture,* with one critical difference: Medina includes discussions regarding the role of religion and spirituality in building a new society. Despite the progress of Western civilization in economic, scientific, and other areas, a lack of corresponding progress with respect to spiritual life has left much of society feeling disoriented and unbalanced. Medina's insight sheds light on ways to address this imbalance. The ultimate goal of this examination is to present a path toward a prosperous global civilization that fulfills humanity's physical, psychological, and spiritual needs.

Paris Talks:
Addresses Given by 'Abdu'l-Bahá in 1911
'Abdu'l-Bahá
$12.00 U.S. / $15.00 CAN
Trade Paper
1-931847-32-0
978-1-931847-32-2

This collection of inspiring and uplifting talks documents an extraordinary series of public addresses 'Abdu'l-Bahá gave on his historic trip to the West in the early twentieth century. Despite advanced age and poor health, he set out from Palestine in 1911 on a momentous journey to Europe and North America to share the teachings and vision of the Bahá'í Faith with the people of the West. Addressing such subjects as the nature of humankind, the soul, the Prophets of God, the establishment of world peace, the abolition of all forms of prejudice, the equality of women and men, the harmony of science and religion, the causes of war, and many other subjects, 'Abdu'l-Bahá spoke in a profound yet simple manner that transcended social and cultural barriers. His deep spiritual wisdom remains as timely and soul-stirring as it was nearly a century ago. 'Abdu'l-Bahá, meaning

Servant of the Glory, is the title assumed by 'Abbás Effendi (1844–1921)—the eldest son and appointed successor of Bahá'u'lláh, the Prophet and Founder of the Bahá'í Faith. A prisoner since the age of nine, 'Abdu'l-Bahá shared a lifetime of imprisonment and exile with his father at the hands of the Ottoman Empire. He spent his entire life in tireless service to, and promotion of, Bahá'u'lláh's cause and is considered by Bahá'ís to be the perfect exemplar of the Faith's teachings.

Partners in Spirit:
What Couples Say about Marriages that Work
Heather Cardin
$12.00 U.S. / $15.00 CAN
Trade Paper
1-931847-31-2
978-1-931847-31-5

Partners in Spirit examines how a marriage can flourish in present-day society when the institution of marriage is seen by many as outdated and unnecessary. Heather Cardin incorporates interviews with over twenty married couples who share what has worked to strengthen their union during their years together. Their stories, hints, and advice illustrate the Bahá'í perspective of marriage, which involves an equal partnership in the spiritual development of both husband and wife. This provides a strong foundation for a happy and prosperous family life. The couples' advice on how to create these spiritual foundations can help both prospective marriage partners as well as those who have been married for years.

The Summons of the Lord of Hosts:
Tablets of Bahá'u'lláh
Bahá'u'lláh
$14.00 U.S. / $17.00 CAN
Trade Paper
1-931847-33-9
978-1-931847-33-9

The Summons of the Lord of Hosts brings together in one volume several major letters written by Bahá'u'lláh, prophet and founder of the Bahá'í Faith. In these magnificent documents he invites the monarchs and leaders of his time to accept the basic tenets of his Faith, sets forth the nature of his mission, and establishes the standard of justice that must govern the rule of those entrusted with civil authority. Written between 1868 and 1870, the letters call upon leaders of the East and West to accept Bahá'u'lláh's teachings on the oneness of God, the unity of all religions, and the oneness of humanity. Among the leaders specifically addressed are Napoleon III, Czar Alexander II, Queen Victoria, Náṣiri'd-Dín Sháh, and Pope Pius IX. A vitally important resource for those interested in the scripture and history of the world's great religions.